THE UL

C2C (

SEA TO SI

EXCELLENT BOOKS

EXCELLENT BOOKS
94 BRADFORD ROAD
WAKEFIELD
WEST YORKSHIRE WF1 2AE
TEL: (01924) 315147
E-mail : peace_richard@hotmail.com
Website : www.excellentbooks.co.uk
Printed 2011

ISBN 978-1-901464-17-7

Whilst the author has researched the route for the purposes of this guide, no responsibility can be accepted for any unforeseen circumstances encountered whilst following it. The publisher would, however, welcome any information regarding any material changes and any problems encountered.

Front cover photos: Top left - C2C start, Whitehaven.
Top right - C2C finish, Tynemouth beach. Bottom - Viewpoint climbing out of Nenthead towards the highest point on the route.
Rear cover photos: Top - Riverside route under the Tyne bridges at Newcastle. Bottom - Castlerigg Stone Circle, Keswick.

Printed by Martins the Printers, Berwick-upon-Tweed, UK

Contents

National Cycle Network - North

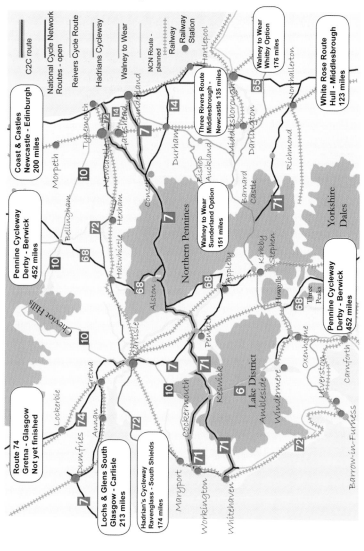

Legend:
- C2C route
- National Cycle Network Routes - open
- Reivers Cycle Route
- Hadrians Cycleway
- Walney to Wear
- NCN Route - planned
- Railway
- Railway Station

Coast & Castles
Newcastle - Edinburgh
200 miles

Pennine Cycleway
Derby - Berwick
452 miles

Route 74
Gretna - Glasgow
Not yet finished

Lochs & Glens South
Glasgow - Carlisle
213 miles

Hadrian's Cycleway
Ravenglass - South Shields
174 miles

Walney to Wear
Whitby Option
176 miles

White Rose Route
Hull - Middlesbrough
123 miles

Three Rivers Route
Middlesbrough - Newcastle
135 miles

Walney to Wear
Sunderland Option
151 miles

Pennine Cycleway
Derby - Berwick
452 miles

Foreword

The C2C was the first National Cycle Route ever to be opened by Sustrans. This was in 1994 and its success was such that we immediately went on to initiate, in 1995, the whole of the National Cycle Network secure in the knowledge that if good routes are created then the public will start to cycle again.

The C2C is just such a route – it is a challenge for many, it has memorable sections through magnificent countryside, it takes the cyclists away from traffic over difficult sections in West Cumbria, Keswick and County Durham, and it has our first collection of milepost sculpture. By now, 16 years on, well over 150,000 coast to coast crossings have been made and many, many millions of pounds put into the local economies along the route.

Even more than this, the C2C route demonstrates that we have a wonderful countryside which can be especially enjoyed by bicycle. Tourism does not have to fill local roads with cars, but rather by cycling the visitor can appreciate the local, distinctive terrain, weather, views, places all the more, and all without damaging, congesting or polluting on the way.

I hope that everyone who uses this guide to explore this wonderful coast to coast route, will then be inspired to cycle more holidays – try the Trans Pennine Trail coast to coast, Glasgow to Inverness through the Highlands, Ilfracombe to Plymouth for a southern coast to coast, Cardiff to Holyhead for a Welsh sea to sea, or even Cowes to Sandown on the Isle of Wight, if you only have a day!

And then be confident to travel more lightly on your day to day journeys, so as make your own personal contribution to a sustainable future for this fragile world we all live in.

John Grimshaw
Founder and former Chief Executive SUSTRANS

C2C & National Cycle Network Signing

The map opposite shows the National Cycle Network throughout the North of England. For those not already familiar with this multi-million pound project, it is made up of traffic-free paths and minor roads (many traffic-calmed) reaching all parts of the UK. The C2C typifies the qualities of the NCN; high quality cycling and walking routes criss-crossing the country that even extend across major urban centres (Sunderland and Newcastle in the case of the C2C). Signed and mapped, it offers a safe, attractive network and a great amenity for cyclists, walkers and people with disabilities. All major routes are identified by route number - as indicated on the map opposite - and several sections of these routes are linked up to form the C2C. Route 71 will carry you to Penrith where you pick up route 7, which you can follow all the way to Sunderland. To get to Newcastle and Tynemouth split off at Consett and follow a combination of NCN routes 14 and 72 (route 72 is part of Hadrian's Cycleway). You will pick up route 1 after passing North Shields ferry, route 1 leading to Tynemouth and along the coast. You may also see signs after North Shields for route 10 in brackets signifying you are heading towards this route. Don't worry though, you won't have to memorise these numbers; the C2C is well signed. Also look out for the milepost markers, just some of the 1,000 along the Network (they are all marked on Sustrans' interactive mapping service found on their website at **www.sustrans.org.uk**). This guide has been designed for use alongside the official Sustrans C2C route map, so with the two you should have all the information required for this ride of a lifetime.

Left: Lamppost stickers in Newcastle
Centre: Direction signing at Rowland's Gill
Right: Milepost as you enter Sunderland

5

Introduction

WHAT IS THE C2C ?

The C2C can fairly claim to be the most popular and most widely known long distance cycle route in the UK, completed by many thousands of people each year. It is to cycling what the Pennine Way is to walking. The longest option runs for around 140 miles across the northern edge of the Lake District, across the Eden Valley and across the beautifully bleak Northern Pennines before dropping down to the post-industrial landscape of the North-East. There are optional starting points (Whitehaven or Workington) and a choice of end point (Tynemouth or Sunderland).

The route uses a mix of specially constructed cycle paths, off-road tracks and minor roads, only occasionally straying onto short sections of main road where necessary. Waymarked along its length, it can be completed by the whole gamut of cyclists, whilst not being designed for any specific sub-group of the cycling world, such as mountain-bikers or tourers. Although undoubtedly a challenge, containing several serious climbs, it is completed by those with little experience of cycling and committed bikers alike. Careful choice of alternative sections should allow just about any type of bike to complete the route (tricycles may have difficulty passing around barriers and on some climbs). However, having a wide range of gears will be a godsend and avoid much uphill pushing.

Why so popular? The C2C was the brainchild of Sustrans, the UK's leading sustainable transport charity, which has promoted the C2C as a 'flagship' long-distance route and it has undoubtedly tapped a demand for long-distance cycle holidays. Some first-rate support facilities have developed around the route. This desire to escape the traffic on two wheels is surely a reaction against the road congestion that has become one of the great logistical and health problems of our age. Many previous non-cyclists have successfully attempted this challenging route and have become more regular cyclists. Another vital area of Sustrans' cycling work, alongside promotion of recreational routes is the promotion and creation of better cycling facilities in urban areas. The C2C has also become extremely popular with charity rides and can fairly claim to have played a major part in raising huge sums for a wide range of charities.

The C2C takes in fantastic scenery. The mountains of the Lake District yield to the subtler but equally beautiful Eden Valley, around Penrith. A very stiff climb up Hartside onto the rolling Pennines provides a further contrast. Settlements are relatively few hereabouts and winter weather can be the most extreme on the whole route. Former lead mining settlements such as Allenheads provide opportunities for sleep and refreshment whilst the landscape also bears reminders of the defunct lead mining industry in the form of old shafts, flues and numerous other constructions. Although the north-east is known perhaps too much for unemployment as a result of heavy industrial decline, it has splendid visitor attractions and remarkable architecture, for example in Newcastle city centre.

The Wearmouth and Tyne bridges, in Sunderland and Newcastle respectively, and the Gateshead Millennium Bridge, are fittingly dramatic heralds to the two finishing points. It's hardly surprising, then, that after negotiating two of the country's main mountain ranges and at least one major city, and linking the Irish and North Seas in the process, a real sense of achievement in completing this epic journey is just about inevitable!

GETTING THERE AND AWAY

The route is designed to be tackled west to east to take advantage of the prevailing wind which means Whitehaven or Workington is the start point for the vast majority who complete the C2C. For rail access see the National Cycle Network - North map at the beginning of the guide. Both the phoning and booking system for rail services, especially when wanting to take bikes, can be complex, no doubt due to the massive reorganisation of the railway system in recent years. At the time of press the system was as follows:

● To take a bike on inter-city services (e.g Leeds to Carlisle) you are definitely advised to reserve in advance but there is normally no extra charge.

●Two companies operate between Carlisle and Newcastle, Scotrail and Northern Rail (who also go on to Sunderland). With the former it's a good idea to book in advance. Northern Rail, who also operate on the line between Carlisle and Workington/Whitehaven, allocate bike space on a first-come, first-served basis. Neither company charges and neither will carry tandems, tricycles, motorised cycles or trailers. Cyclist busy line.

●Once you know your travel times it is advisable to check with the relevant company. To get to a main line you may have to use your regional railway and therefore you will need to make a similar check as to their arrangements. Train company websites can be found via **www.nationalrail.co.uk** where you can also check train times and book tickets.

National Rail Enquiry Service (Inter-city routes) 08457 484950
Northern Rail Sales 08457 000125
Scotrail Sales 08457 550033 Customer relations 0845 6015929

●Useful leaflet "Cycling by train" produced by Brompton and available at railway stations or downloadable from www.nationalrail.co.uk. It gives the cycle carriage rules position of each company and phone number. See also www.atob.org.uk
●Trains from Tynemouth to Newcastle are part of the Newcastle Metro system and do not take bikes other than folding bikes. It is therefore necessary for non-folders to retrace your tracks back to Newcastle Central station. If heading back to Whitehaven from Sunderland you'll have to cycle or get the train back to Newcastle.

Easy cycling along the Whitehaven-Ennerdale section of the C2C

A number of companies offer combinations of motorised back-up, package holidays on and around the C2C, accommodation booking and luggage transfer:

Adventure Cycling - Fully guided bespoke rides
07736816700 www.adventurecycling.co.uk
The Bike Bus - cycle collection / delivery. Stanley Taxis, Stanley
(01207) 237424 www.bikebus.uk.com sales@ukcyclingholidays.com
Coast to Coast Holidays and Baggage Service - return transport, luggage transfer, package holidays and accommodation booking service.
Tel / fax (01642) 489173 www.coasttocoast-holidays.co.uk
CycleActive - offer regular self-guided and guided trips throughout spring, summer and autumn along the C2C - accommodation, bag transfer, route information, extra loops for mountain bikers, breakdown support and return transport from the finish. Flexible itineraries available for groups. (01768) 840400 www.cycleactive.co.uk
Cycle Transport North East - motorised transport for bikes and luggage, up to 64 passengers (01388) 818284 www.coasttocoastbikes.co.uk
Discovery Travel - offer self-guided four, five or six night holidays Whitehaven to Sunderland (01904) 632226 www.discoverytravel.co.uk
Glaramara Guest House - Keswick. Cumbria Way Cycle Route - (72+ miles, Ulverston - Carlisle) two day alternative to the C2C with route guide and accommodation (on C2C route). Bags / cycle transport available. Cycle activity weekends in Lake District (brochure). Bike hire available. (017687) 73216 / 75255 www. cumbriawaycycleroute.co.uk and www.keswickcycleactiveguesthouse.co.uk keswick.9glaramara@virgin.net
Haven Cycles - 500m from C2C start. Secure, insured car parking, car delivery to finish point, baggage transfer, cycle hire, minibus service with cycle trailer, on route cycle repairs and recovery. Services also available for Hadrian's Wall, Reivers and other local routes. 01946 63263
www.havencycles-c2cservices.co.uk havencycles@gmail.com
Saddle Skedaddle - offer both supported and self-guided trips on the C2C amongst their range of UK, European and long haul holidays (0191) 2651110 www. skedaddle.co.uk info@skedaddle.co.uk
The Bicycle Transport Co. - bespoke transport for bikes and people (01207) 240400 www.thebicycletransportcompany.co.uk
The Sherpa Van Project - provides an accommodation booking service, a daily baggage carrying service and transport for bikes and passengers back to their start point, on the C2C and other footpaths and cycle trails. www.sherpavan.com or call (0871) 5200124
Trailbrakes - 3 day self-guided holidays on the C2C
07922 653327 www.trailbrakes.co.uk
Tyne Valley Holidays - longstanding firm offering backup services and run by Ted Gillman. No longer offering the service as Ted retired in 2011.

HOW LONG SHOULD I TAKE?
How long you allow yourself depends on experience, fitness and choice of route. Although some ultra-fit enthusiasts aim to do the whole route in less than 24 hours, the vast majority of C2Cers are holidaying and usually take between three and seven days. Some keen cyclists, especially those with previous experience of the route, complete it over a long weekend. Most people seem to go for three days to complete the route in reasonable comfort but without too much in the way of sightseeing or diversions. For a more leisurely experience allow four days or more.

This guide is split into five 'day' sections, ranging from 22 to 31 miles, aimed at novice cyclists or those with plenty of time who want to take in some attractions, with section start and finish points at or near major population centres to ensure plenty of accommodation and other services.

For two-day trips Garrigill and Alston make good overnight stops if you're doing well, or even Nenthead if you're really moving. They're just beyond the half way stage and have a good amount of accommodation - this will give you a much easier second day. If you would rather save the climb to Hartside for day two, accommodation seems to peter out after about Renwick.

For three-dayers there are plenty of places to stay in and between Keswick and Penrith for night one. Places between Allenheads and Castleside all have accommodation for night two but as the second half of the route is easier, it may not stop you finishing the journey as planned if your second night is around Alston or Nenthead. Four-day trips and beyond introduce countless permutations of how the journey can be split up. A not too recent survey suggested that overall Keswick and Nenthead were the most popular overnight halts. With the right preparation and conditions, the C2C can be whatever sort of route you want to make it - a strenuous challenge route through to a leisurely recreational route. Do have a realistic idea of what daily mileage you are comfortable achieving; remember that the C2C has a large range of terrain and difficulty, from the considerable challenge of the Old Coach Road alternative to flat cyclepaths, so adjust time estimates accordingly. The route descriptions and profiles at the beginning of each section of this book give a good idea of what to expect.

WHEN SHOULD I GO?
The route is designed to be useable all year round although a winter trip will need more care and planning and may not be advisable if the weather does not promise well. Potentially extreme weather conditions mean you should be particularly wary of crossing the Penrith to Nenthead section between November and April. Weather forecasts should be taken into account whatever the time of year. Good detailed Met Office forecasts for ten days can be had by phone from Weathercall: Cumbria and Lake District 09068 500419 Durham, Northumberland and Tyne & Wear 09068 500418 but they are 60p a minute from a landline and can take a while. Good websites for forecasts are www.metoffice.gov.uk and www.bbc.co.uk/weather. All these will provide temperature, wind direction, visibility, outlook and more. George Fisher - www.georgefisher.co.uk - the outdoor store in Keswick has a live webcam view of conditions in Keswick.

It is advisable to book accommodation as far in advance as practicable, especially in summer or if you are planning to stay in smaller settlements with only limited accommodation. Some accommodation providers,usually in the very busy spots such as Keswick, or at very busy times such as bank holidays may have minimum stay requirements of more than one night.

Those wanting to camp along the way should certainly have some previous cycling experience and allow extra time as the extra weight slows down even the fittest cyclist quite noticeably.

Whatever time of year you're going, be prepared - typically, it rains on about one day in three in England, probably more in The Lake District and Pennines. The higher you go, the more likely it is to be cold and windy and there's always the possibility of hill fog. Poor weather is one of the two things most often cited in a 2000 survey as most detracting from enjoyment of the route. If you are in a position to plan very short-term, it may well help.

Country lanes don't come much more idyllic and quiet than this; approaching Wythop Woods on section 1B

C2C FACTS FROM 2002 SURVEY

- 69 % of users surveyed were travelling east.
- Most got to the route by bike - only 8% came in a car.
- All were there for leisure purposes - 44% as part of a holiday.
- Average age was 38.
- 85% were male.
- The average amount of cycling in a day was 6.1 hours.
- The majority of users were regular, experienced cyclists but 25% were occasional cyclists including a few new to the activity.

Thanks to Andy Cope of Sustrans for the above.

OTHER C2C FACTS

- A 4 year old has completed the C2C in 3 days. He pedalled a 'tagalong' bike attached to his dad's cycle. It was completed both for fun and as a fund raising effort for a cancer charity in memory of the little boy's mother who died from the disease.
- Doing the C2C in a day is a challenge for only the fittest and most serious of cyclists. The quickest time we have heard of is around 12 hours - an average of around 11 miles per hour cycling continuously or 12 miles per hour with an hour's food break.
- The C2C has been completed by Brompton folding bike (a six speed version in the account we read). Perhaps the craziest group of all succeeded in completing the route on large-wheeled unicycles!

1A Whitehaven - Keswick

Route Info

31 miles / 50 km
Off - road 12 miles / 19 km
Accumulated distance 31 miles / 50 km

After a bit of fiddly navigation out of Whitehaven centre the Whitehaven - Ennerdale cycle path provides a gentle start, passing by several former iron mining villages. The route initially follows the line of a disued rail network that served a myriad of local mines. The true mountains of the Lake District are soon in sight, heralded by pleasant villages such as Lamplugh and High Lorton as you dip and climb on quiet minor roads. The moderate climb after Kirkland village will warm you up ready for the steep but spectacular climb over the Whinlatter Forest. After a twisting off-road descent on wide forest tracks the quaint villages of Braithwaite and Portinscale are accompanied by easy pedalling on quiet roads to Keswick where you should beware of the brief but busy A-road section into the centre.

Descending towards the Vale of Lorton

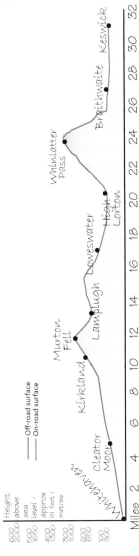

11

WHITEHAVEN TO LORTON Start by slipway of inner harbour by the C2C sculpture. Traditional to dip your wheel in the sea! After turning up Quay St. go right onto Swingpump Lane and across the mini-roundabout at its end onto New Town, then over another mini-roundabout onto Preston Street and very shortly turn left onto a tarmac path. Beware of staggered junction of path shortly as it crosses a road. Under railway turn off path onto Esk Avenue and then rejoin path by infants school. Briefly exit path onto Croasdale Avenue then Wasdale Avenue. Rejoin path to head out of the town.

Follow the well-surfaced traffic-free trail ignoring any exits. Don't be confused by yellow coast to coast walking route signs - this is not your route! To exit the traffic-free trail bear right near the West Cumbria Field Centre, through the trees. Turn left onto the road through the wooden arch. Stay on this road and head straight through the small village of Kirkland and stay right at the set of junctions after Felldyke, following Loweswater signs into Lamplugh. Following Loweswater signs will take you past Loweswater lake before bearing left before Loweswater village.

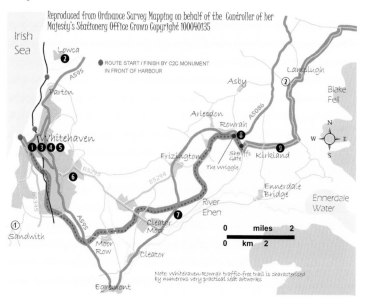

Reproduced from Ordnance Survey Mapping on behalf of the Controller of her Majesty's Stationery Office Crown Copyright 100040135

● ROUTE START / FINISH BY C2C MONUMENT
IN FRONT OF HARBOUR

Note: Whitehaven-Rowrah traffic-free trail is characterised by numerous very practical seat artworks

LORTON TO KESWICK Coming into Low Lorton bear right then left at the staggered crossroads over the B5289. Keep on this road out of High Lorton and start to climb very steeply to join the B5292 for a short while. Look out for the turning right onto a wide forest track on the right, then immediate left. This track then parallels the B road (ignore any right turns) before dropping down to meet the B road again near the top of Whinlatter Pass. Go left then right to enter Whinlatter visitor centre. Just behind the main building of the visitor centre bear right. Descend the steep and bendy forest track to the road and head right into Thornthwaite.

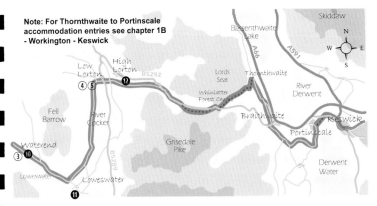

Note: For Thornthwaite to Portinscale accommodation entries see chapter 1B - Workington - Keswick

Bear right onto the very minor road through Lanefoot Farm (easy to miss) and follow this road back over the B road to Ivy House and straight through Braithwaite centre. Follow signs for Ullock on this very minor road, through Ullock and into Portinscale where you bear right by Derwentwater Hotel and cross the river via a footbridge. Head right onto the B road (BEWARE OF TRAFFIC) and right onto the even busier A591 into Keswick centre.

NAVIGATION TIPS
* The above direction tips will help you navigate but we strongly advise using the official Sustrans map (latest edition) along with this guide.
* See www.c2cplaces2stay.co.uk for online details of accommodation and much more and www.sustrans.org.uk/map for route updates
* The route is signed along much of its length but don't rely purely on signs - check your location against this guide and the Sustrans map.

Hotels and Guesthouses

WHITEHAVEN

❶ GLENARD GUEST HOUSE Inkerman Terrace Whitehaven CA28 7TY
(01946) 692249 💻 www.glenard.co.uk   info@glenard.co.uk
From £30.00 Locally approved 🍴 ⊺drying room 🚲 ✗
Open all year 🚶0.25mile

❷ GLENLEA HOUSE Stamford Hill Lowca Whitehaven CA28 6PS (01946)
693873 💻SEA386@aol.com From £25 🛏11 Locally approved
Snacks all day Licensed bar 🍴on request ⊺ drying room ⊡on request
🚲24 ✗ Open all year 🚶3 miles from Whitehaven on Whitehaven to
Workington link route

❸ LISMORE   28 Wellington Row Whitehaven CA28 7HE (01946) 66028
💻pamcliffdixon@btopenworld.com £28.00-30.00   🛏1d1s3t1f
Locally approved 🍴 🚲 Open all year 🚶0.5 miles

❹ THE TIVOLI GUEST HOUSE   156 Queen Street Whitehaven CA28 7BA
(01946) 67400   💻 www.tivoliguesthouse.co.uk £33.00 Locally approved
🍴 24hrs notice ⊺drying room & radiators ⊡£2.00 🚲20 🚌 ✗
Hose available Open all year 🚶approx 800 metres from start

❺ THE WAVERLEY HOTEL 13-14 Tangier Street Whitehaven CA28 7UX
(01946) 694337 💻 www.thewaverleyhotel.co.uk £30.00 - £32.00 Locally
approved 🍴 🍴 ⊺ 🚲 Open all year 🚶100 yards

❻ CROSS GEORGIAN GUEST HOUSE Sneckyeat Road Hensingham
Whitehaven CA28 8JQ (01946) 63716 💻 thecross@ukonline.co.uk £20.00
- £25.00 🛏1d1t1s1f Locally approved 🍴 ⊺ ⊡on request 🚲 Open all
year Parking facilities for those leaving cars and returning 🚶1 mile from start

WHITEHAVEN TO KESWICK

❼ THE PARKSIDE HOTEL Parkside Road, Cleator Moor CA25 5HF
(01946) 811001 💻www.parksidehotelcumbria.co.uk From £27.50 🛏1t,2tr,1f
en suite, 1t,1tr. 🍴Lunches. Full evening bar meals menu. Real ales 🍴
⊺ drying facilities - tumble driers 🚲 🚌 rider pick-up if stuck/pre-arranged
drop-off Open all year 🚶on the route

❽ THE STORK HOTEL Rowrah Road Rowrah CA26 3XJ (01946) 861213
💻www.storkhotel.co.uk £35.00 🍴restaurant 🚶0.5 miles

❾ ENNERDALE VIEW B & B Looking Steads Kirkland CA26 3XY (01946)
862311 💻www.ennerdale-view.co.uk £30.00 🛏1s,2d en suite 1t Locally
approved 🍴 notice night before ⊺ drying room - radiators - heaters - full
central heating   🚲4 Hose available for bike washing. Close to Rowrah
Cart and Mini Motor racing Club 1 mile from Coast to Coast walk
Open all year 🚶100m

⑩ ASKHILL FARM Loweswater CA13 0SU (01946) 861640 £32.00
🛏 1f 1tr ♦♦♦ 🍽 evening meal £15.00-£19.00 special diets catered for 🍽
🍵 ♿ ⚒ Hose available Open February to October 🚶on route

⑪ KIRKSTILE INN Loweswater CA13 0RU (01900) 85219
🖥 www.kirkstile.com info@kirkstile.com £48.50 🛏 7d4t ♦♦♦♦
🍽 Full menu every lunch & evening 🍽 🍵 Drying room ♿ Open all year
Real ale inn - microbrewery started 2003 🚶1 mile

⑫ MEADOW BANK High Lorton CA13 9UG (01900) 85315
🖥 www.buttermerecumbria.com £28.00 🛏 1t en-suite 1d Locally
approved 🍽 🍵 ♿ ⚒ Open all year Pub nearby 🚶300 yards

Hostels and Campsites

① TARN FLATT BARN Tarn Flatt Hall Sandwith Whitehaven CA28 9UX
(01946) 692162 or 758198 🖥 www.tarnflattfarm.co.uk £8.50 per person per
night Locally approved Sleeps twelve in camping barn ▲ Camping also
available 🍽 breakfast bookable in advance 🍵 ♿ Long stay car parking
available Open all year 🚶3 miles

② INGLENOOK CARAVAN PARK Lamplugh CA14 4SH (01946) 861240
▲ 6 Tent and cyclist £12.00 per night. Flush toilets Hot showers Shop
▫ Open all year 🚶On route

③ SWALLOW BARN Waterend Farm Loweswater CA13 0SU (01946) 861465
or (01946) 758198 🖥 www.lakelandcampingbarns.co.uk £8.50 🛏 3 x 3
persons & 1 x 9 persons ▲ 5 YHA approved 🍽 none but pub nearby ♿10
Pressure hose available Water heater Two showers (coin operated) Open
all year 🚶on route

④ WHEATSHEAF INN Low Lorton CA13 9UW (01900) 85199
🖥 www.wheatsheafinnlorton.co.uk ▲ Parking available for support vehicles
Toilets, showers, washing and drying facilities Open March - November
🚶400 yards

⑤ WHINFELL HALL FARM Low Lorton CA13 0RQ (01900) 85260 ▲30
£6.00 per pitch Toilets & showers ♿ Open March - October 🚶on route

**Note: For Thornthwaite to Portinscale accommodation
entries see chapter 1B - Workington - Keswick**

Food and Drink

1. STORK HOTEL Rowrah Road Rowrah CA26 3XJ (01946) 861213
🖳 www.storkhotel.co.uk Real ale bar with restaurant serving breakfasts, lunches and evening meals. 🕍 ⛴Adjacent to route

2. THE HOUND INN Arlecdon CA26 3XE (01946) 862162 Drinks only during day and restaurant meals in the evening John Smiths and Jennings ☁️
⛴0.5 miles

3. KIRKSTILE INN Loweswater CA13 0RU (01900) 85219
🖳 www.kirkstile.com info@kirkstile.com Full meals, baguettes, jacket potatoes. Real ale pub - Yates, Jennings, Coniston Bluebird, Melbreak (own brewery) ☁️ ⛴1 mile

4. WHEATSHEAF INN Low Lorton CA13 9UW (01900) 85199
🖳 www.wheatsheafinnlorton.co.uk Lunch 12-2 Evening meal 6-8.30
Closed Mondays Snacks to full menu and vegetarian £5-£10 Jennings
Beer garden ⛴400 yards

5. SISKINS CAFE Whinlatter Forest Visitor Centre CA12 5TU (017687) 78410 Open seven days - 10.00 - 5.00 Range of hot and cold drinks, soups, sandwiches, jacket potatoes etc. specials of the day. ⛴on the route

Bridge seats sculpture, Whitehaven - Ennerdale railpath

Visitor Attractions

WHITEHAVEN Listed **'Gem Town'** with well-preserved Georgian architecture. Unusual gridiron street pattern. The first planned town since the middle ages. Many fine buildings. See Roper St. and Lowther St. for good examples. Interesting **harbour area** with nearby mine remains of Wellington and Duke Pits at South Beach Recreation Area. Focus of multi-million pound regeneration scheme with lighting scheme and sculptures. **Candlestick Chimney viewpoint** part of former Wellington pit (operating 1840-1932). Scene of 1910 mine disaster with 136 lives lost. The **Beacon Museum** showing the town's connection with slavery, smuggling, mining, shipbuilding and America. Met. Office **weather gallery** and views over the Solway Firth. Admission charge. (01946) 592302. **Michael Moon's Bookshop**, Lowther St. - huge selection of 2nd hand books. **St. James' Church** has a fine Georgian interior. **St. Nicholas' Church** consists of a fine tower on Lowther St. (drinks and snacks some weekends). **Haig Colliery Mining Museum** is situated high on the cliffs above Whitehaven. The Steam Winding Engine is normally operated daily (01946 599949). **Rum Story** on Lowther Street has lots of interactive exhibits about the town's trade and sells rum. (01946) 592933.

CLEATOR MOOR Modern miners memorial sculpture in market square at Cleator Moor as well as Stirling Memorial to former mine owner. Cleator Moor was known as Little Ireland because of the many Irish immigrants who settled here after the 19th century Irish potato famine. Iron ore mining was the main industry and the cycle path you have come here on once took thousands of tons of ore to Whitehaven harbour.

LOWESWATER Gorgeous village of scattered houses and farms, lying between the smallest of the Lakes, Loweswater and Crummock Water in a spectacular location, Large agricultural show every September.

LOW AND HIGH LORTON Picturesque villages marking the start of your ascent into the Lake District proper. Situated in the flat green Vale of Lorton and surrounded by Lakeland peaks. Lorton Hall has a fifteenth century pele tower and George Fox, the founder of the English Quaker movement, preached behind the High Lorton village hall.

WHINLATTER FOREST VISITOR CENTRE (017687) 78469 Run by the Forestry Commission and open 7 days 10.00 - 4.00 weekdays and 10.00 - 5.00 weekends Shop sells confectionery etc. Exhibition centre with good displays for all ages Two mountain bike trails in the Forest, a 19km red grade and a 7.5km blue grade. Bike hire at Cyclewise shop. Nice walks also. Go Ape is a treetop adventure assault course. Picnic sites Siskins cafe - see food and drink section Set of cycle racks ⚲on route

For Braithwaite and Portinscale entries see chapter 2.

Whinlatter Forest, with its many waymarked trails, is a haven for off-road riders.

Bike Shops

HAVEN CYCLES 2 Preston Street Whitehaven CA28 9DL
(01946) 63263 💻 www.havencycles-c2cservices.co.uk
havencycles@gmail.com Secure, insured car parking, car delivery to
finish point, baggage transfer, cycle hire, minibus service with cycle trailer,
on route cycle repairs and recovery. Services also available for Hadrian's
Wall, Reivers and other local routes. 🚲on the route 500 metres from the
start.

AINFIELD CYCLES, Jacktrees Road, Cleator Moor CA23 3DW
(01946) 812427 💻 www.ainfieldcycles.co.uk Repair service, sales & cycle
hire (you can pick up a bike here in Cumbria and drop it off in the north-
east). Call-out service when possible 🚲Approx 1 mile. On the minor road
between Cleator and Cleator Moor, just north of Cleator.

CYCLEWISE WHINLATTER, Whinlatter Forest Park, Braithwaite CA12 5TW
(017687) 78711 💻 www.cyclewise.co.uk Trailhead shop offering sales,
bikehire, workshop, bike wash and a range of MTB training courses.

Tourist Information

WHITEHAVEN TOURIST INFORMATION Market Hall Market Place CA28 7JG
(01946) 598914 💻 www.western-lakedistrict.co.uk

MARKET DAYS Thursday and Saturday

Descending out of Whinlatter Forest gives spectacular views
across the flood plain around Keswick and on to Lakeland peaks

You are soon out of Whitehaven and onto easy traffic-free riding

Whinlatter Forest

1B Workington - Keswick

Route Info

Section Distance 25 miles / 40 km
Off-road 6 miles / 10km

Accumulated Distance 25 miles / 40km

Workington is still a working port and the harbour area is still dominated by heavy industry. Despite losing out to Whitehaven in this respect the section has advantages; it is shorter and with more gentle gradients and offers the chance to visit the lovely historic market town of Cockermouth. There is some moderate climbing between Cockermouth and Wythop Woods but a very steep descent awaits through Wythop Woods, with spectacular glimpses of Bassenthwaite Lake ahead. Take great care here and dismount if in any doubt. Careful navigation also required on the network of forest tracks. A relatively easy road section through Thornthwaite follows as you unite with the alternative start route from Whitehaven. Take care as you have to mix with busy traffic coming into Keswick.

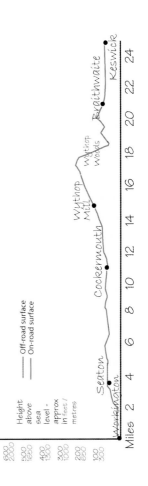

Approaching Wythop Woods on a sunlit upland plateau

21

WORKINGTON - COCKERMOUTH In 2009 floods destroyed many of the bridges in West Cumbria. Most have been rebuilt, but Workington is the exception. At the time of writing the disused rail bridge on older C2C maps has gone completely, and the main road bridge closest to the sea has yet to be re-built. However, there's a temporary road bridge upstream, and another of the original bridges further east is in use.

There is a new route signed on the ground which is cycleable, though not ideal. Signposts (some misleading) lead the cyclist through car parks on to a main road before going back to the original route north of the river. Neither the official C2C map nor the Sustrans website is quite right. Signed C2C (at time of writing) and our suggested route are shown below:

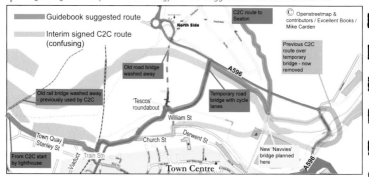

Stay on the tarmac cycle track out of Workington, all the way to Camerton (leave the railpath at Uplands, just before a bridge crosses it). In Camerton turn left, signed Great Broughton 2¼. Stay on main road through Great Broughton following Cockermouth signs. Descend out of village then turn left signed Papcastle, 1¾. Ignore left for Carlisle in Papcastle.

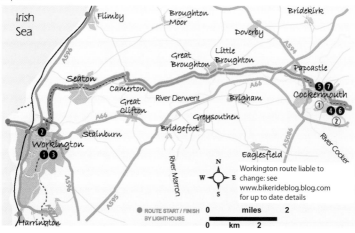

COCKERMOUTH - KESWICK Descend the hill to Cockermouth and cross Gote Road onto rubbly, rough path. Turn right then left and cross over the bridge to Bridge St. Left down Main Street, cross the bridge into Market Place; right fork, then immediate right into car park – tourist info directly in front; turn right –going past Rannerdale/Bike Ride Shop office – following road into the riverside car park to far end; cross footbridge and turn left. Under the viaduct turn right up the hillside, alongside a row of terraces. At T-junction go right and cross over viaduct onto the traffic-free trail. Stay on the track, crossing road, past cemetery. Hairpin round edge of cemetery to road opposite Strawberry How Business Centre and left onto road.

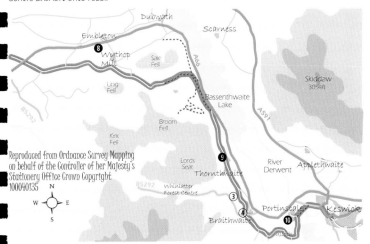

Reproduced from Ordnance Survey Mapping on behalf of the Controller of her Majesty's Stationery Office Crown Copyright 100040135

Follow road into Wythop Mill then turn right and climb. Turn right by farmhouse. Straight through gate onto farm track. Bear right at the split and then into Wythop Woods. Follow the narrow rocky descent and cross straight over a wider, good quality track, staying on minor path. At the bottom of the slope right onto minor road and straight through bus turning circle onto old section of tarmac road. Turn right at road junction and into Thornthwaite. Bear right onto the very minor road through Lanefoot Farm (easy to miss) and follow this road back over the B5292 to Ivy House and straight through Braithwaite centre. Follow signs for Ullock on this very minor road, through Ullock and into Portinscale where you bear right by Derwentwater Hotel and cross the river via a footbridge. Head right on the B road and then a busy A road into Keswick.

NAVIGATION TIPS
* The above direction tips will help you navigate but we strongly advise using the official Sustrans map (latest edition) along with this guide.
* See www.c2cplaces2stay.co.uk for online details of accommodation and much more and www.sustrans.org.uk/map for route updates
* The route is signed along much of its length but don't rely purely on signs - check your location against this guide and the Sustrans map.

Hotels and Guesthouses

WORKINGTON

❶ MORVEN GUEST HOUSE Siddick Road Workington CA14 1LE (01900) 602118 ⌨ www.morvenguesthouse.com info@morvenguesthouse.com £33.00 - £34.00 ⮑ 4t2d(can be let as singles) ♦♦♦ Early breakfast on request 🍽£5.00 ⊺drying room ⮢20 🛠can supply basic tools Open all year ⛽ on route near start

❷ OSBORNE HOUSE 31 Brow Top Workington CA14 2DP (01900) 603400 £25.00 ⮑5t1f Locally approved 🍽£4.00 please ask day before ⊺radiators and electric heaters ⊡ ⮢ Pressure hose available Open all year ⛽0.75 miles

❸ SILVERDALE 17 Banklands Workington CA14 3EL (01900) 61887 £26.00 ⮑2t2s Locally approved ⊺tumble dryer and Aga ⮢ 🛠tools available Open all year ⛽0.5 miles from start of route

COCKERMOUTH

❹ GRAYSONSIDE Lorton Road Cockermouth CA13 9TQ (01900) 822351 ⌨www.graysonside.co.uk From £40.00 No one night bookings on Saturday, bank holiday weekend or in high season. ⮑3d1t1fourposter-all en suite Locally inspected-commended 🍽 no, but hotel across road with bar food and restaurant meals 🍽 ⊺ ⊡ ⮢ Hose for washing bikes down Tennis court Self-catering apartment also available Open all year ⛽approximately 1 mile on B5292 just past A66

❺ THE ROOK GUEST HOUSE 9 Castlegate Cockermouth CA13 9EU (01900) 828496 ⌨www.therookguesthouse.gbr.cc/ £25.00 ⮑2d1t Locally approved 🍽 ⊺radiators and tumble drier ⊡washing machine ⮢6 Open all year ⛽300 yards

❻ ROSE COTTAGE Lorton Road Cockermouth CA13 9DX (01900) 822189 ⌨ www.rosecottageguest.co.uk bookings@rosecottageguest.co.uk £32.50-£40.00 ⮑4d3t2f ♦♦♦♦ 🍽dinner £20.00 🍽 ⊺drying room ⊡next day service charged accordingly ⮢20 Closed three weeks in February ⛽half a mile

❼ SIX CASTLEGATE GUESTHOUSE Cockermouth CA13 9EU (01900) 826786 ⌨www.sixcastlegate.co.uk From £37.50 ⮑1s2f1d (en suite) 2d 1t 🍽 ⊺drying room ⮢ Open all year ⛽200 yards

EMBLETON

❽ ORCHARD HOUSE Embleton CA13 9XP (017687) 76347 ⌨www.slee-cottage.co.uk £30.00 ⮑2d1d/t Locally commended Non smoking 🍽 breakfast only - vegetarian and other diets can be catered for 🍽 notice night before ⊺drying room ⮢ 🛠 Hosepipe for washing down 🚗 by prior arrangement Restaurant and pub within a quarter of a mile Self catering cottage also available - weekly rates, short breaks available in winter Open all year ⛽half a mile

APPROACHING KESWICK

❾ POWTER HOWE Thornthwaite Keswick CA12 5SQ (017687) 78415
£25.00 ⤚2d1t2s Locally approved ▮ ⌐ ⊛plenty of space Sixteenth
century Tudor statesman's farmhouse in three acres of gardens Views over
Bassenthwaite Lake towards Skiddaw Open all year ⚑on route

❿ THE MOUNT Portinscale nr. Keswick CA12 5RD (017687) 73970
⌨ www.mountkeswick.co.uk £42.00 one night only / £36.00 for two or more
nights ⤚3d1t1s Locally approved ▮(24hrs notice) ⌐ ⊛6 ✗basic tools
🚌 arrangeable through Sherpa / other companies at a charge Self catering
cottage also available on weekly basis Tearoom (summer) and restaurant / bar
nearby Open all year ⚑50 metres

Hostels and Campsites

① COCKERMOUTH YOUTH HOSTEL Double Mills Cockermouth CA13 0DS
(01900) 822561 / 0845 371 9313 ⌨ www.yha.org.uk cockermouth@yha.
org.uk Adults £14.00-16.00 U18 £11.00 ⤚1 x 4 persons, 1 x 10 persons
and 1 x 12 persons (26 beds) ✱✱(hostels) ▮Self-catering kitchen available
⌐drying room ⊛15+ ✗basic tool kit Open to individuals April to Sept
inclusive - open to groups booked in advance rest of year Camping available
⚑approximately half a kilometre

② GRAYSONSIDE Lorton Road Cockermouth CA13 9TQ (01900) 822351
⌨www.graysonside.co.uk stay@graysonside.co.uk ⛰6 £7.50pp Shower
and toilet block ▮breakfast available in farmhouse to campers - booking
required ⊛ Open beginning of April to end of October
⚑approximately 1 mile on B5292, just past A66

③ LANEFOOT FARM CAMPSITE Thornthwaite CA12 5RZ (017687) 78097
/ 78567 ⌨www.stayinthornthwaite.co.uk ⛰about 50 (in a glorious setting)
£7.50 low season £8.50 high season per person per night (minimum of 2
nights, 3 at bank holidays) . Toilets. Showers. Hot and cold washing-up
facilities. ⌐drying room ⊛ Electric hook-up available. Self catering cottages
also available Food in nearby Braithwaite. ⚑on route

④ SCOTGATE HOLIDAY PARK Braithwaite CA12 5TF (017687) 78343
⌨www.scotgateholidaypark.co.uk ⛰150 From £9.70 (1 person 1 tent low
season. Minimum stay periods at busy times. No advance bookings for tents).
Toilets and showers Shop and cafe ▢ Open 1st March to beginning of
November ⚑ on route 10 minutes walk from the main site is Braithwaite
Bridges, Scotgate's woodland campsite.

Food and Drink

GREAT BROUGHTON Brewery House pub. (01900) 824698
COCKERMOUTH has a great range of restaurants and pubs and you will be
spoilt for choice. The **Bitter End** pub on Allerdale Court with its own microbrewery you can view as you drink a local brew or have a meal.
Vegetarians might like to try **Quince and Medlar** at 13 Castlegate where the
emphasis is on quality vegetarian food.

Visitor Attractions

WORKINGTON Although more of a working town than Whitehaven,
Workington still has its attractions and there are plenty of pubs and restaurants
should you choose it as a start point. The **Helena Thompson Museum**
(01900) 606155 / 64040 is based around local collections. Includes social and
industrial history of Workington, once world famous for coal, ship building and
steel. Housed in a fine Georgian building. Free admission. Park End Road.
Workington Hall is an imposing ruin and former home of local Lords of the
Manor the Curwens who built up the local coal industry. Full cork model in
Helena Thompson Museum. Hall closed to public but grounds and parkland
open.

CAMERTON Pretty church on banks of Derwent.

GREAT BROUGHTON **Christ Church** is a pretty village church.

PAPCASTLE Former site of a Roman fort, now a pleasant village.

COCKERMOUTH   One of only two listed 'Gem Towns' in Cumbria
(Whitehaven is the other). Extremely **pretty market town** with interesting
nooks and crannies and without the large numbers of tourists that towns
nearer the centre of the Lake District attract. **Wordsworth House** was the
home of William and Dorothy Wordsworth. National Trust owned. Admission
fee to non-members. Seasonal variations in opening. (01900) 820884. Statue
of R.Mayo in main street. Former town MP and only Viceroy of India ever
assassinated. **Jennings Brewery Tour**. Working brewery. Admission charge.
0845 1257190 **Castlegate House** is an art gallery and sculpture garden
based around northern and Scottish artists. The **Sheep and Wool Centre**
has three-hundred seat arena with the chance to see sheep dogs in action
and 19 different breeds of sheep. It also houses the **Cumwest Exhibition**
with background on the Western Lakes and is found on Egremont Road to the
south of the centre (01900) 822673.

Approaching the C2C start in Workington

Bike Shops

THE BIKE BANK   6 Market Place Workington CA14 4AX (01900) 603337
Full repair and sales service.   About 0.5 miles from route, in town centre.

HALFORDS SUPERSTORE (01900) 601635 Derwent Howe Retail Park
Workington CA14 3YW Spares and repairs   Approx 1 mile south of the
route

4 PLAY CYCLES (01900) 823377 25 Market Place Cockermouth CA13 9NH
Repairs & sales   Call out when possible   Cycle hire
  Just off the route as it passes through Cockermouth

Tourist Information

WORKINGTON VISITOR INFORMATION POINT Workington Library,
Vulcans Lane CA14 4ND (016973) 31944   www.western-lakedistrict.co.uk

MARKET DAYS Wednesdays & Saturdays

COCKERMOUTH TOURIST INFORMATION Town Hall Market Street CA13 9NP
(01900) 822634   www.western-lakedistrict.co.uk

Minor country lane at Thornthwaite on your approach into Keswick

2 Keswick - Penrith

Route Info

22 miles / 35 km
Off - road 5 miles / 8 km
Accumulated distance from
Whitehaven 53 miles / 85 km
from Workington 47 miles / 75 km

The high summits of the Lake District are left behind as you approach the flatter more pastoral country of the Eden Valley, with its accent on quiet market towns and glorious woodlands contrasting with the large-scale tourism of the Lake District. Although the main route is relatively flat the off-road option along the Old Coach Road is a serious challenge as the exposed rocky track climbs high onto Threlkeld Common, whilst the main route gently undulates along the valley bottom. The other off-road alternative is the delightful and generally very easy Keswick railway path. After a couple of gradients it turns into a leisurely pedal through thick woods, crossing and re-crossing the River Greta over a series of charming bridges to bring you to the picturesque village of Threlkeld. There are then some beautiful and generally very lightly trafficked roads to Greystoke, whether you take the Berrier or the Troutbeck option. The gated road up to Mungrisdale is delightful with great views of surrounding peaks. More minor roads and tracks bring you through Newton Reigny to Penrith, avoiding any of the major roads that converge on the town.

Approaching the Old Coach Road

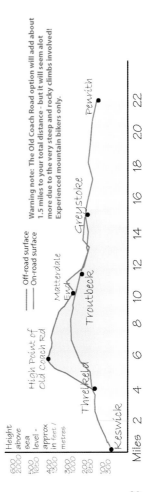

Warning note: The Old Coach Road option will add about 1.5 miles to your total distance - but it will seem alot more due to the very steep and rocky climbs involved! Experienced mountain bikers only.

—— Off-road surface
—— On-road surface

High Point of Old Coach Rd

Matterdale End

Troutbeck

Greystoke

Penrith

Threlkeld

Keswick

Height above sea level - approx in feet / metres

600 / 2000
500 / 1650
400 / 1300
300 / 1000
200 / 650
100 / 300

Miles 2 4 6 8 10 12 14 16 18 20 22

KESWICK - GREYSTOKE   You enter Keswick on the main road and follow Bank Street and Station Road to the car park by the swimming pool and the start of the railpath to Threlkeld. The railpath passes over the river and the main road. Continue under two more main roads using the impressive stilted boardwalk which has now replaced the old and troublesome steps over the former railway tunnel. Continue on this delightful track for another couple of miles before bearing left on the road into Threlkeld. Through Threlkeld join the cycleway alongside the A66 for a mile or so then pick up the road at Scales to head up and down the Glenderamackin valley (Mungrisdale village worth a look). Join another section of cycleway by the A66 then from Troutbeck it is easy navigation on quiet minor roads to Greystoke.

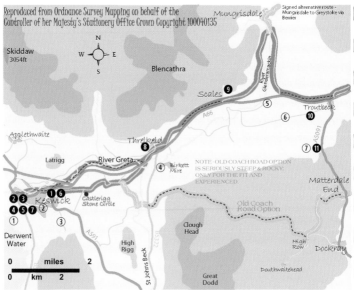

CASTLERIGG STONE CIRCLE / OLD COACH ROAD OPTION You will need to exit the Keswick-Threlkeld railpath as it first passes under a main road. After briefly joining the main road take the right onto a minor road signed for Castlerigg Stone Circle and climb steeply to this wonderful ancient site. Over Naddle Beck you then have the option to descend back to the main route at Threlkeld or carry on climbing via Shundraw, to the start of the Old Coach Road just over the B5322. Navigation on this option is not difficult - but it is a real physical test!

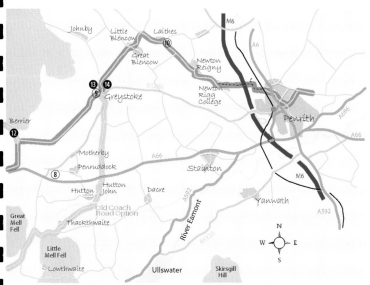

GREYSTOKE - PENRITH Head into Greystoke village centre and in front of Greystoke Castle follow signs for Johnby and Blencow. It is now easy navigation through the villages of Little Blencow, Laithes and Newton Reigny. About half a mile out of Newton Reigny turn left at the Millennium Milepost and pass through the university buildings at Newton Rigg, using the public bridleway link to come under the M6 bridge. Turn right at a T-junction here and follow the track under the railway. The track becomes Robinson Street and at the end you cross a main road onto Drovers Lane. Follow this road for about 150 yards, over a roundabout, then head right down Hunter Lane towards Penrith centre. If by-passing the town centre ignore Hunter Lane and carry straight on down Meeting House Lane to pass the bus station and head left up Fell Lane.

NAVIGATION TIPS
* The above direction tips will help you navigate but we strongly advise using the official Sustrans map (latest edition) along with this guide.
* See www.c2cplaces2stay.co.uk for online details of accommodation and much more and www.sustrans.org.uk/map for route updates
* The route is signed along much of its length but don't rely purely on signs · check your location against this guide and the Sustrans map.

31

Hotels and Guesthouses

KESWICK

❶ ASH TREE HOUSE Penrith Road Keswick CA12 4LJ (017687) 72203
www.ashtreehouse.co.uk ⊠ peterredfearn@AOL.com £25 - £30
⌀2 rooms Locally approved ⦿ ⌂ ♿ Open all year
Car park to rear - room for major support vehicle
🚆few hundred yards from the main route (on Castlerigg alternative route)

❷ BECKSIDE GUEST HOUSE 5 Wordsworth Street Keswick CA12 4HU
(017687) 73093 ⊟www.beckside-keswick.co.uk info@beckside-keswick.
co.uk From £32.00 ⌀3d2t1f Locally approved ⦿ ⌂ ♿ ✗for
minor repairs Family guest house run by experienced cyclists Open all year
🚆300 metres

❸ GLARAMARA GUEST HOUSE 9 Acorn Street Keswick CA12 4EA
(017687) 73216 mobile 07711 763 019
⊠www.keswickcycleactiveguesthouse.co.uk www.cumbriawaycycleroute.
co.uk keswick.9glaramara@virgin.net £30.00 ⌀2d2t (en suite) 1s
Locally approved ⦿snack menu
⦿ from £4.50 flasks from £1.50 - ask night before ⌂radiators, airers and
drying racks in rooms ⊡laundrette 100yards away ♿10 ✗basic tools and
minor repairs - OTC qualified mountain bike leader 🚌 up to 6 bikes and
cyclists. Emergency pick-up / collection Cycle hire available
Cycle activity weekends / mid-week breaks - see page 8 for details
Open all year 🚆400 yards

❹ GLENCOE GUEST HOUSE 21 Helvellyn Street Keswick CA12 4EN
(017687) 71016 ⊠ www.glencoeguesthouse.co.uk
enquiries@glencoeguesthouse.co.uk From £32.00 ♦♦♦♦ ⦿request
when booking ⌂ drying room, heaters and radiators ⊡laundrette opposite
guest house ♿ ✗assistance with repairs - guest house run by cyclists
Pressure hose Open all year 🚆0.25 miles

❺ GRASSMOOR GUEST HOUSE 10 Blencathra Street Keswick CA12 4HP
(017687) 74008 Non-smoking ⊠www.grassmoor-keswick.co.uk
info@grassmoor-keswick.co.uk £32.00 ⌀4 rooms all available as twin,
double or triple - 2 family rooms ♦♦♦ ⦿ ⌂drying room and tumble dryer
⊡clothes wash and DIY iron ♿10 ✗workshop with comprehensive tools
and bike tools Hosepipe for washing down 🚌 people, luggage & bike
recovery Open all year 🚆100 metres

❻ IVY LODGE 32 Penrith Road, Keswick CA12 4HA (017687) 75747
⊠www.ivy-lodge.com From £30.00 ⌀2f1d/t Locally approved ⦿ ♿8
✗ basic tools Hosepipe for washing down Open all year 🚆on route

❼ RIVENDELL 23 Helvellyn Street Keswick CA12 4EN (017687) 73822
🖥 www.rivendellguesthouse.com £33.00 min. 3-night stay on bank holidays
🛏 s,d,t and triples - most en suite Can accommodate up to 15. Locally
approved ⊤drying room ⬚ ♻12 ✗workshop facilities Pressure hose
🚌 ask when booking   Open all year 🚶on route near town centre

KESWICK TO PENRITH

❽ THE HOLLIES Threlkeld Keswick CA12 4RX (017687) 79216
🖥www.theholliesinlakeland.co.uk info@theholliesinlakeland.co.uk
£37.00 (Friday or Saturday £39.00) 🛏4d/t en suite ♦♦♦♦ ⬤ ⊤drying room
⬚ ♻8 Hose for washing bikes   Open all year 🚶on route at Threlkeld

❾ SCALES FARM COUNTRY GUEST HOUSE Scales Threlkeld CA12 4SY
(017687) 79660 🖥 www.scalesfarm.com scales@scalesfarm.com
£35.00 (supplement for single night and minimum stay periods)
🛏3d2t1f all en suite ♦♦♦♦ ⬤ ⊤drying room ♻ 1st April to 1st Nov
🚶on route

❿ GILL HEAD FARM Troutbeck Penrith CA11 0ST (017687) 79652
🖥 www.gillheadfarm.co.uk From £30.00 (single night supplement) 🛏5
rooms (some family) ♦♦♦ ⬤guests' kitchen with prepared evening meal
service ⬤ ⊤radiators tumble dryer ⬚coin operated washer ♻ ✗
Pressure hose for bike washing   Open March to November 🚶on the route

⓫ RIVERSIDE FARM HOLIDAYS Troutbeck Penrith CA11 0SS
(017684) 80970 / 07966 486701 🖥 www.riversidefarmholidaycottages.co.uk
From £25.00 ⬤ ⊤clothes hangers ⬚£2 ♻ ✗ Pressure hose for
bike washing All year 🚶on the route

Taking a break at the old station platform before setting off on
the railpath to Keswick.

⑫ WHITBARROW FARM Berrier CA11 0XB (017684) 83366
🖳 www.whitbarrowfarm.co.uk   mary@whitbarrowfarm.co.uk
£37.50 - £45.00   ⚲ 2t/d1d   ♦♦♦♦   🍽 no but two pubs nearby   🍽 ↑
⌴   🚲 Pressure hose on request   Open all year   🚶500 yards

⑬ ORCHARD COTTAGE Church Road Greystoke Penrith CA11 0TW
(017684) 83264   £28.00 - £30.00   ⚲ 1f (en suite) 1d (private bathroom)
Locally approved   🍽   ↑   ⌴   🚲   ✗   Open April - October
🚶on route

⑭ STAFFORD HOUSE Greystoke Penrith CA11 0TQ
(017684) 83558 🖳 www.stafford-house.co.uk £35.00   ⚲ 1t 2d Also self-
catering lodges - one for 5 people, other for 10 at £25 pppn (cooked breakfast
available but extra in lodges). Shop and pub with food nearby.   Open April -
October   🚶on route

Hostels and Campsites

① CAMPING AND CARAVANNING CLUB SITE Crow Park Road Keswick CA12
5EP (017687) 72392 🖳www.campingandcaravanningclub.co.uk ⛰250 £7.65
- £9.15 per person per pitch per night and £5.60 - £6.50 per backpacker per pitch
per night - advance booking recommended - minimum booking periods on standard
pitches - non-members welcome, additional fees ✱✱✱✱and 3 pennants Gold
David Bellamy Conservation Park Award   Toilets & showers ↑ ⌴ Open February
- November 🚶approx 0.5 miles

② KESWICK YOUTH HOSTEL Station Road Keswick CA12 5LH 0845 371 9746
🖳www.yha.org.uk £20.40   ⚲1x2 persons 7x3 persons 7x4 persons 2x5 persons
4x6 persons (85 beds) all rooms can be used for family groups ✱ ✱ ✱ ✱ 🍽breakfast
£4.95 Evening meal Self catering available   🍽 ↑drying room ⌴washer, dryer and
ironing facilities   Open all year   🚶on route

③ CASTLERIGG FARM CAMPING AND CARAVAN SITE Keswick CA12 4ET
(017687) 72479 🖳www.castleriggfarm.com ⛰£5.50 to £6.70 pppn Reservations not
taken for tents ✱ ✱ ✱ ✱ Toilets and showers ↑tumble dryer ⌴washing machine and
iron 🚲 Hose for washing bikes Cafe for breakfast and evening meals Quiet site
with great views Open mid-March to mid-November 🚶quarter of a mile

④ SETMABANNING FARM Threlkeld CA12 4TT (017687) 79229 ⛰30 Toilets
Showers ↑ 🚲 Open March to October   🚶0.5 miles

⑤ HUTTON MOOR END CARAVAN SITE The Stables Troutbeck Penrith CA11
0SX (017687) 79149 🖳www.campingandcaravanningclub.co.uk ⛰27 £7.25-
£8.48 per person plus a pitching fee (discounts for CCC members) - prices are
backpacking (ie non-car) rates Toilets Showers Small shop ↑tumble dryer
CCC site Open March to mid-November 🚶less than a mile

⑥ GILL HEAD FARM Troutbeck Penrith CA11 0ST (017687) 79652 ▢www.
gillheadfarm.co.uk ▲ from £7.50pp Camping pods from £35.00 per night (min
2 nights at weekends) AA 2 pennants Toilets Showers ⌐tumble dryer ▢coin
operated washer ♻ ✗ Pressure hose for bike washing Shop Camping pods
are timber built, insulated wooden huts designed to be used like a tent. Contact
site for further info. Open Easter to November 🚲on the route

⑦ RIVERSIDE FARM Camping & Caravanning Club Certificated Site (joining
available on site) Troutbeck Penrith CA11 0SS (017684) 80970 / 07966 486701
▲50 From £5 Toilets & showers, wash down facilities, garden furniture,
chimineas ▢ ♻ 🚲Approx 1.3 miles

⑧ BECKSES CARAVAN & CAMPING PARK Penruddock Penrith CA11 0RX
(017684) 83224 ▲10 From £5 Toilets & showers ♻ March - Oct
🚲 200 metres

⑨ GREYSTOKE CYCLE CAFE CA11 0UT (017684) 83984 ▢www.
greystokecyclecafe.co.uk Basic facilities only i.e. toilet and washroom and
camping in the garden 🚲on the route

⑩ TOWN END COTTAGE CARAVAN CLUB SITE & CAMP SITE Laithes Penrith
CA11 0AW (017684) 84317 Fax (017684) 84458 ▲5 £3.00 per tent per night
(two people) Toilets NB - no showers, cold water only available Indoor and
outdoor swimming pools three miles away Pub three quarters of a mile Quiet
rural site on the edge of the Lake District National Park Open all year
🚲 on route

STAFFORD HOUSE at Greystoke (see ⓮ opposite) do camping by prior
arrangement).

The Keswick-Threlkeld
railpath explores some
beautiful wooded valleys

Visitor Attractions

BRAITHWAITE Attractive village with pubs and a village store, which does sandwiches (www.braithwaitegeneralstore.co.uk) set in lovely surroundings.

PORTINSCALE Elegant villa settlement next door to Keswick despite its name deriving from the Norse for prostitute's hut! Pub.

KESWICK Established as a mining centre and market town, it quickly became a Victorian tourist centre due to its setting amidst glorious Lakeland scenery. Remains the main **tourist centre** in the Northern Lakes. A number of interesting buildings include the **Moot Hall** (tourist info. building) and **Crosthwaite Church** with panoramic viewfinder. Southey's grave and consecration crosses inside and outside the building. **Keswick Museum and Art Gallery** has an interesting and unusual collection of objects in a traditional museum setting. (017687) 73263 **Pencil Museum** (017687) 73626 World's longest pencil and other offbeat pencil information **Derwentwater Boat Trips** Calling at the main points of interest around the lake - ring Keswick Launch on (017687) 72263. **George Fisher** Huge stock of outdoor activity goods on Borrowdale Rd.

CASTLERIGG STONE CIRCLE On a hilly route option out of Keswick but a fantastic 3,000 year old stone circle amidst the towering hills. Despite the hordes who visit in summer it still has the aura of a very special place, especially as we don't really know why ancient man performed what must have been backbreaking work to move the stones here.

THRELKELD Former mining community with TB sanitorium built nearby. **Threlkeld Quarry and Mining Museum** (017687) 79747 Off the B5322 south of the route in the old quarries. Huge geology book collection for sale. Easter to Oct.

MUNGRISDALE An alternative signed route goes via Mungrisdale and Berrier to Greystoke. The very basic style of the church of **St Kentigern** suits this lonely outpost.

GREYSTOKE Compact centre based around village green. Impressive entrance to private castle and market cross. Interesting 13th century church. *Tarzan of the Apes* modelled on Lord Greystoke. Village has own public swimming pool. Local pottery and art gallery add to the charm. Note local Cycle Cafe entry opposite (campsite entry too).

BLENCOW Before entering Blencow look for the hall on the left with modern house built into ruined defensive pele towers.

Resting at
an idyllic spot in
Greystoke
village

Food and Drink

BRAITHWAITE **Coledale Inn*** CA12 5TN (017687) 78272 💻www.coledale-inn.co.uk Lunchtime and evening meals. £5-£10 Range of local and other beers. Vegetarian options. Children's meals. Outside seating area. **Royal Oak Inn*** CA12 5SY (017687) 78533 💻www.royaloak-braithwaite.co.uk Lunch 12-2 Bar meals 6-9. £5 and up. Jennings ales and other real ales. Locally based ingredients.

KESWICK As you might expect of the main town of the northern Lakes, Keswick has a large number of eateries from fish and chips to a la carte. **Lakeland Pedlar,** Hendersons Yard CA12 5JD (017687) 74492, a stone's throw from the route, has vegetarian wholefood in a cafe above the bike shop. For those who want 'cyclists' fuel' try the **Cornish Pasty** at 3 Lake Road CA12 5BS. **Maysons Cafe and Restaurant** on Lake Road CA12 5DQ comes recommended by C2Cers.

THRELKELD Two good pubs; **Horse & Farrier*** CA12 4SQ (017687) 79688 💻www.horseandfarrier.com (bar food all day, restaurant 12-9) and **Salutation Inn*** CA12 4SQ (017687) 79614 💻www.thesalutation.co.uk (12-3 & 6-9) both offer a good range of bar meals and welcome cyclists. The latter boasts steak and ale pie!

TROUTBECK **Troutbeck Inn*** CA11 0SJ (017684) 83635 💻www.troutbeckinn.co.uk A good range of bar meals.

GREYSTOKE **Greystoke Cycle Cafe & Tea Garden** CA11 0UT (017684) 83984 Easter to end of Sept 10-6 for cyclists. Home baked cake, speciality teas and coffees, soups, light vegetarian lunches but also bacon butties and beans on toast. Snacks and a drink from under £5.

BLENCOW **Crown Inn** CA11 0DG (017684) 83369 Bar meals 7-9 Mon-Sat. Lunches 12-2 Sundays £5 - £10.

NEWTON REIGNY **The Sun Inn** CA11 0AP does meals (01768) 867055

* These also offer accommodation.

Probably the single hardest section on the C2C; the Old Coach
Road option has amazing views on a clear day

Bike Shops and Other Facilities

IAN HINDMARCH, next to village store, Braithwaite. Fixes bikes.
(017687) 78273

GLARAMARA GUEST HOUSE CYCLE HIRE, 9 Acorn Street Keswick
CA12 4EA Also spares and repairs. (017687) 73216/75255 . On C2C
B5289 section, coming into Keswick.

KESWICK MOUNTAIN BIKE CENTRE, Southey Hill CA12 5LE
www.keswickbikes.co.uk (017687) 74407 / 75202 Bike hire. Accredited
Shimano repair centre 0.25 miles

LAKELAND PEDLAR BICYCLE CENTRE, Hendersons Yard, Keswick CA12 5JD
(017687) 75752 www.lakelandpedlar.co.uk Spares & repairs A stone's
throw from the route in Keswick town centre. Also includes wholefood and
vegetarian cafe

Mountain bikes are for hire at Keswick Leisure Pool (017687) 72760.

Tourist Information

KESWICK TOURIST INFORMATION Moot Hall, Market Square CA12 5JR
(017687) 72645   www.keswick.org www.lake-district.gov.uk

MARKET DAY Saturday

3 Penrith - Nenthead

Route Info

27 miles / 44 km
Off - road 5 miles / 8 km (optional)
Accumulated distance from
Whitehaven 80 miles / 129km
from Workington 74 miles / 119 km

Leave Penrith behind on a long,
steady climb up to some spectacular
Lakeland views from Beacon Edge.
Be careful joining a brief section of
B then A road before the village of
Langwathby. Leaving the gentle Eden
Valley behind, you soon climb steeply
to the spectacular viewpoint of
Hartside ('extreme' off-road options
up to here for those who like that
sort of thing) before beginning the
traverse of the Northern Pennines,
'England's Last Wilderness', much of
it designated an Area of Outstanding
Natural Beauty. Though lacking
the alpine quality of the lakes,
the sombre, wide open spaces
present, if anything, a more powerful
landscape and there are certainly
fewer settlements and chances for
refreshment. The off-road option
between Garrigill and Nenthead is a
challenge but good fun; two waterfalls
and some very steep, rocky rough
stuff suitable for more experienced
off-roaders only. You should be
aware of potentially extreme
weather conditions if crossing this
part of the route November - April.

Off-road option to Hartside

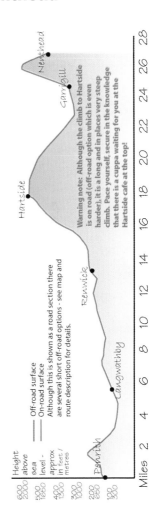

39

PENRITH - LANGWATHBY The C2C takes a complicated loop through Penrith centre- Follow Hunter Lane past the police station and take the last left to bring you out on the main street. Go left here along the main street up to the Monument clock then left again on the path between Natwest and Barclays (dismount here). After 150 yards go left into Sandgate and right in 50 yards after the car park. Head to mini-roundabout and right then almost immediately take a left onto Fell Lane. Climb Fell Lane and go right onto Beacon Edge. Take the first left turn off Beacon Edge and descend down a steep hill to the B6412 (beware sharp left halfway down). In less than half a mile go right to meet the main A686 and left into Langwathby. Take the first left off the main road in Langwathby and pass the post office and church to exit the village.

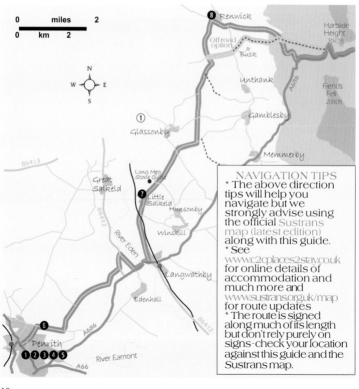

NAVIGATION TIPS
* The above direction tips will help you navigate but we strongly advise using the official Sustrans map (latest edition) along with this guide.
* See www.c2qplaces2stay.co.uk for online details of accommodation and much more and www.sustrans.org.uk/map for route updates
* The route is signed along much of its length but don't rely purely on signs - check your location against this guide and the Sustrans map.

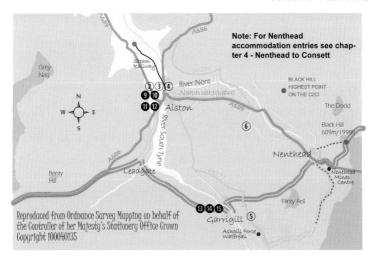

Note: For Nenthead accommodation entries see chapter 4 - Nenthead to Consett

Reproduced from Ordnance Survey Mapping on behalf of the Controller of her Majesty's Stationery Office Crown Copyright 100040135

LANGWATHBY TO NENTHEAD Follow the road out of Langwathby and in 1½ miles climb steeply through Little Salkeld (detour to Long Meg to left 1 mile out of Little Salkeld - worth a visit). Back on the main route head over the next crossroads and descend for ½ a mile before taking a road on the left for Renwick which crosses Viol Moor. Another couple of miles on this road brings you to Four Lane End, heading straight on to Renwick (right at Four Lane End is the off-road option which then crosses Five Road Ends, becoming increasingly rough and steep). Bear right in Renwick for the minor road approach to the A686 and left. From Hartside viewpoint you simply follow the A686 east and take the first right to descend to the tiny settlement of Leadgate. Bear right here on a lovely undulating road, along the side of the valley and into Garrigill. For the road option go left at the village green and across the River South Tyne. In about 100 yards go sharp right and climb steeply over the side of Flinty Fell. Descend steeply into Nenthead where a sharp right takes you to the village centre.

For the off-road option keep on past the green as you enter Garrigill and in 150 yards or so head left across the river via a ford to a very steep, rocky ascent. At the top turn right onto the B6277 then in a mile or so, just after the spectacular waterfall of Ash Gill Force head left to climb through forest then descend and bend left across another ford onto a rocky moorland track to bring you to Nenthead Mines Centre. Straight on into Nenthead centre.

ALSTON ALTERNATIVE

Navigation is a cinch - over Hartside follow the main A686 to Alston and from there pick up the A 689 to Nenthead. Note you will encounter some fast traffic as you would expect on A roads, especially in the holiday season.

Hotels and Guesthouses

Note: For Nenthead accommodation entries see chapter 4 - Nenthead to Consett

PENRITH

❶ ACORN GUEST HOUSE   Scotland Road Penrith CA11 9HL
(01768) 868696 ⌨ www.acorn-guesthouse.co.uk £34.50-£50.00 ⇦3d3t1f
•••• ◉ ◉ ⌐ ⊡ laundry room includes tumble dryer ⚙ Open all year
⚲ on route

❷ ALBANY HOUSE 5 Portland Place Penrith CA11 7QN (01768) 863072
⌨ www.albany-house.org.uk info@albany-house.org.uk
From £35.00 ⇦3d1t1f ••••   warm welcome award ◉ ⌐and central heating
always on ⊡wash and dry if required ⚙12 ✕   Open all year   ⚲ on route

❸ BRANDELHOW GUEST HOUSE   1 Portland Place Penrith CA11 7QN
(01768) 864470   ⌨ www.brandelhowguesthouse.co.uk £35.00
⇦2f3t3d1s •••• ◉ ⌐ ⚙ ✕cycle shop within 100 yards   Hose available
🚲 by negotiation   Open all year   ⚲ on route

❹ BROOKLANDS GUEST HOUSE 2 Portland Place Penrith CA11 7QN
(01768) 863395   ⌨ www.brooklandsguesthouse.com £37.50 per person
⇦5d4t2s1f ••••• ◉ ⌐ ⊡ ⚙ Pressure hose for bike washing Closed
Christmas Bike hire and cycling holidays available through CycleActive
⚲ on route

❺ CALEDONIA GUEST HOUSE 8, Victoria Road CA11 8HR (01768) 864482
⌨ www.caledoniaguesthouse.co.uk   £34.00 ⇦2d3t1f •••• ◉ ⌐ tumble
dryer - heaters in rooms ⊡ washer and dryer ⚙ Open all year ⚲ 100 yards

❻ ROUNDTHORN COUNTRY HOUSE Beacon Edge Penrith CA11 7HA
(01768) 863952 ⌨ www.roundthorn.co.uk £62.50 ⇦ 10d/s3f/triple •••••
◉ supper menu - range of prices ◉   ⌐ ⊡ ⚙ ✕ Open all year   ⚲ on route

PENRITH TO ALSTON

❼ BANK HOUSE FARM Little Salkeld Langwathby CA10 1NN (01768) 881257
⌨ www.bankhouseequestrian.co.uk B&B from £30.00 pppn ⇦self-catering or
B&B in static caravans ◉ ⚙ Open all year   ⚲ on route

❽ SCALEHOUSE FARM Scalehouses Renwick CA10 1JY (01768) 896493
⌨ www.scalehousefarm.com From £30.00 Dormitory bunk bed accommodation
also available ⇦2d1t ◉ evening meal from £14.00 ◉ £5.00 notice needed
⌐ drying room and tumble dryer ⊡ small charge ⚙ ✕ ⚑Camping possible
(use of shower and toilet) Last stop before ascent to Hartside   Open all year
⚲ 1 mile

ALSTON ALTERNATIVE

❾ CUMBERLAND HOTEL Townfoot Alston CA9 3HX (01434) 381875
💻 www.alstoncumberlandhotel.co.uk   HelenguyH@aol.com
£35.00   🛏2t2d1f   🍽two course dinner from £7.50 per person
🍽   ⊤dryer   🚲15   Open all year   C2C stamping point
🚶 on Alston alternative route

❿ HARBUT LAW Brampton Road Alston CA9 3BD (01434) 381950
💻 www.cumbria-cottages.co.uk   thomas@younger.fsnet.co.uk
£30.00   🛏1fen suite 1d en suite 1d private Locally approved
🍽   ⊤   ⊡laundry room with washer, dryer and iron
🚲   ✗basic tools   Open April - October   Self catering also available
🚶 on the A689 alternative route 1 mile out of Alston

⓫ HIGHFIELD Bruntley Meadows Alston CA9 3UX (01434) 382182
💻 kalinkaleo@gmail.com   £25.00   🛏1d/f en suite 1t1s   🍽three course
dinner £10   🍽£3.50 notice on evening of arrival   ⊤drying cupboard and
radiators   ⊡   🚲5   🚌   Open all year   🚶0.25 miles

⓬ ALSTON HOUSE HOTEL Townfoot Alston CA9 3RN (01434) 382200
💻 www.alstonhouse.co.uk   From £50.00   🛏1t1triple4f/d all en suite 🍽l 🍽
⊤ radiators and drying room   🚲20   Luggage forwarding service   Open all
year 🚶 on Alston alternative route

GARRIGILL

⓭ GARRIGILL POST OFFICE GUEST HOUSE Garrigill CA9 3DS (01434)
381257 💻 www.garrigill-guesthouse.co.uk   anne.bramwell@btopenworld.com
From £28.00   🛏2t1d2s   Locally approved   🍽no but pub with meals next
door 🍽   ⊤   🚲   ✗   Open all year   🚶100 yards

⓮ BRIDGE VIEW   Garrigill CA9 3DJ (01434) 382448
💻 www.bridgeview.org.uk   £24.00 per person per night   🛏1 room sleeps
up to three people or a family   🍽evening meal   🍽 from £4.00   ⊤ ⊡
laundry and drying service   🚲 Open all year   🚶on route

⓯ EASTVIEW Garrigill CA9 3DU (01434) 381561
💻 wwwgarrigillbedandbreakfast.co.uk   £26.00   🛏1t 1d   🍽 from £5.00
⊤drying facilities   🚲   Open all year   🚶 on route

43

Hostels and Campsites

① MAINS FARM CAMPSITE Mains Farm Kirkoswald CA10 1DH 01768
898342 ▣ www.edenvalleycaravansite.co.uk ▲5 £12-15 per pitch ⚙
Free hot showers H&C water Toilets Electrical hookup Nearby Kirkoswald
offers village shop, post office and pub. Open all year Also has a bunkhouse -
www.edenvallybunkhouse.co.uk ⚑Approx 1 mile

② ALSTON YOUTH HOSTEL The Firs. Alston CA9 3RW 0845 3719301
▣ www.yha.org.uk alston@yha.org.uk £17.95 adult £14.95 under 18
⌕2 x 2 bedded rooms, 2 x 4 bedded rooms and 3 x 6 bedded rooms ✶✶✶
🍽 evening meal & breakfast Self catering kitchen facilities available 🍽
╦drying room ▢large sink and spin dryer ⚙20 ✗cycle tool kit Open
March/April - October/November 'Escape to...' rest of year ⚑half a mile

③ ALSTON TRAINING AND ADVENTURE CENTRE High Plains Lodge Alston
CA9 3DD (01434) 381886 ▣www.alstontraining.co.uk
alstontraining@btconnect.com ▲5 £4.00 per person Dormitory
accommodation available Bed and breakfast accommodation £21.00
🍽 evening meal 🍽 Self catering facilities available by arrangement ╦
▢by arrangement ⚙ TV, video and pool room Open all year ⚑1 mile

④ TYNE WILLOWS Station Road Alston (01434) 382515 ▲30 £4 per berth
(ie price depends on tent size) ⚙ Free showers H&C water Toilets Co-Op
store nearby Open Easter - November ⚑Approx 200 metres

⑤ Note the village hall in Garrigill is available as a camping barn and has
space for tents. Contact via Bridge View B&B (01434) 382448 or East View
B&B (01434) 381561 for details.

⑥ HUDGILL CARAVAN PARK nr Nenthall, Alston (01434) 381731
£7.00 per tent, £3.50 per extra person Showers and toilets ▢
⚑On Alston alternative loop.

Camping also at Scalehouse Farm, Renwick, see pg 42 for details

Food and Drink

PENRITH Some of the more original choices across a large range are:
James and John Grahams - had enough of butties and flasks? Then try this
long-established and classy delicatessen and take away a selection of delights
opposite the Musgrave monument. Not cheap but delicious. **Purple Sage
Restaurant** offer a C2Cers special of sandwich, soup and filled flask for £4.50.
On the route opposite St Andrews Church. **Alans Cafe**, Poets Walk. Mediter-
ranean and English dishes and a good vegetarian choice. **Ice Cream Garden**,
10 Cornmarket. Tea room and ice cream parlour with, as the name suggests,

a garden. If you are after crafts and homemade food then **Eden Craft Gallery** is adjacent to the C2C as it passes St Andrews Church.

LANGWATHBY **Brief Encounter Cafe** (01768) 881902 at Langwathby Station Open 7 days March to October, 9-5, Nov-Dec 10-4 (closed Mondays). Offers coffee, lunch and afternoon tea ⚹Less than 0.5 miles from the route, in a lovely setting, at Langwathby train station, on the Settle-Carlisle line. **Shepherds Inn** (01768) 881335 Lunches / evening meals daily ⚹Next to route.

THE WATER MILL at Little Salkeld (01768) 881523, is indeed a water-powered mill with a tea room offering organic and vegetarian drinks, snacks and lunches. The flour produced here is used in the bread and cakes available in the cafe. Totally non-smoking. Open daily except over Christmas to mid-January. ⚹Next to the route

MELMERBY village is not on the C2C route but those after organic food might find **The Village Bakery** (01768) 881811 / 898437 worth the detour. This renowned bakery and cafe offers breakfast, coffee, lunch and tea and has a bakery shop. There is also **The Shepherds Inn** (01768) 881741 next to the huge village green, offering lunches and evening meals.

HARTSIDE TOP CAFE (01434) 381036 Lays claim to be England's highest cafe at 1904 feet! Open 7 days, spring and summer. Fri-Mon in winter, but closed all Dec. Much frequented by cyclists and motorbikers.

GARRIGILL **Thortergill Tea Rooms** (01434) 381936   Open 10.00 to 5.00 except Mondays (open bank holidays) early March until late October Soups, sandwiches, ham and egg pie, quiche and homemade cakes with 24 different teas, 11 different coffees and soft drinks Full meal and drink £5.00 - £10.00 Cycles can be left in view outside tearoom window Traditional tearoom with blacksmith's forge, display rooms of forged ironwork and a waterfalls walk ⚹ on route
Garrigill Post Office Take out tea and coffee available from post office shop. There is also the **George & Dragon** (01434) 381293

ALSTON OPTION

ALSTON has loads of eating and drinking holes including tearooms such as **Blueberrys** and characterful inns such as **The Turks Head**, both on the Market Place. The **Moody Baker** is a bakery and shop specialising in wholefood and vegetarian nosh. The **Cumberland Hotel** is a C2C stamping point and has bar meals (see accommodation section for more details).

Visitor Attractions

PENRITH Beautiful red **sandstone market town**, historically the target of Scottish border raids. Series of market places connected by narrow streets show desire for security against the Scots. **Penrith Beacon** is a hilltop structure used through the ages to warn of the threat of invasion. Present structure dates from 1719. Accessible by foot. Signed at junction at top of Fell Lane. **Robinson's School** (01768) 867466 Former charitable provider of education now housing tourist information and small museum. No charge. **St. Andrew's Church** Set in fine architecture of Bishop's Yard. Medieval tower with Georgian nave. Unusual 'Giant's Grave' in churchyard (arrangement of ancient crosses and hogback graves) near Gothic monument to Robert Virtue (railway engineer). **Castle ruins** Begun in the fourteenth century and later occupied by Richard Duke of Gloucester as 'Guardian of the West march towards Scotland'. **Musgrave Monument** Erected 1851 by public subscription as a memorial on the early death of the son of Sir George and Lady Musgrave. Many other **fine buildings** such as the Mansion House and Town Hall. Out of town, about 2 miles south-west of the route you will find **Rheged**, Europe's biggest grass-covered building, housing giant cinema, plenty of shops, restaurants and cafes.

LANGWATHBY AND AROUND Compactly centred around the village green. A couple of miles down the road at **Little Salkeld** there is a nice walk to Lacey's Caves. Water-powered mill produces organic flours (see food and drink section for details). **Long Meg and her Daughters** is an impressive prehistoric stone circle with large megalith at the head. 60 stones of 360 ft diameter. The purpose is unsure but it has possible funerary connections. Little Meg is a smaller circle to the north with no public access. A very short detour from the C2C as it climbs out of Little Salkeld.

HARTSIDE TO GARRIGILL Superb 580m viewpoint after a very tough climb out of the Eden Valley. Cafe by viewpoint. The **North Pennines Area of Outstanding Natural Beauty** is entered after climbing Hartside. Looks and feels barren but harbours a unique blend of flora, fauna (e.g. alpine flowers and birds such as the merlin) and industrial archaeology. The great northern rivers the Tyne, Tees, Wear and Derwent rise here. Several hills are crossed but the area is in fact one massive block of ancient rock, covered mainly in peat, 40 by 36 miles.
Garrigill A very picturesque village based around a village green. Blacksmith's Forge and Waterfalls Walk are on the alternative road route leaving Garrigill (Thortergill - see food and drink for more details). Phone forge before arriving out of season. **Ashgill Force** A fifty foot waterfall near Garrigill you can stand behind. Access on foot only.

ALSTON OPTION Frequently used by C2C riders even when it wasn't on the official map (now a route option on the latest map). It lies at the junction of two 'A' roads and therefore you will have some relatively heavy traffic to face, but there are many facilities here not available in Garrigill or Nenthead. Alston claims to be England's **highest market town** at 280m (919ft). Its greatest period of growth was based on a largely **Quaker-owned lead mining industry**. During its heyday in the nineteenth century the town had a population of 10,000 but is now down to 2,000. Tourism is becoming one of the main industries. Many **old attractive buildings**, mainly nineteenth century attracted the media to make a TV version of Oliver Twist. It is also a regional centre for artists and craftspeople. The **parish church** is one of the most notable buildings, featuring the Derwentwater clock. Greenwich Hospital gained large estates in the area and gave the clock to the church. **South Tynedale Railway**. England's highest narrow gauge railway, running for 2.25 miles along former BR track. 15 minute trip through great scenery. Running hours vary. (01434) 381696. Talking timetable (01434) 382828. The **Nent Force drainage level** began in Alston and was over four miles long when work ceased and took 60 years to build. Became a tourist attraction in the nineteenth century with boat trips and underground dancing! After extraction and smelting the lead was carried away by sturdy Galloway ponies.

Once over the Hartside summit huge rolling moors open out before you

Bike Shops

ARRAGONS 2 Brunswick Road Penrith CA11 7LU (01768) 890344
Spares & repairs. Cycle hire. 🚲 Very near route as it passes through Penrith Centre.

HARPERS 1-2 Middlegate Penrith CA11 7PG (01768) 864475 Spares & repairs. 🚲 Very near route as it passes through Penrith Centre.

HALFORDS Ullswater Road Penrith CA11 7JQ (01768) 892960 Spares & repairs.

Tourist Information

PENRITH TOURIST INFORMATION Robinsons School Middlegate CA11 7PT (01768) 867466 🖥 www.visiteden.co.uk Pen.tic@eden.gov.uk

PENRITH MARKET DAY Tuesday

RHEGED TIC Penrith CA11 0DQ (01768) 860034 🖥 www.visiteden.co.uk

ALSTON TOURIST INFORMATION Town Hall Market Place CA9 3RF (01434) 382244 🖥 www.visiteden.co.uk alstonlocallinks@eden.gov.uk Open daily in summer.

Preparing for the testing climb out of Nenthead to the C2C's highest point

4 Nenthead - Consett

Route Info

29 miles / 46 km
Off - road 16 miles / 26 km
Accumulated distance from
Whitehaven 109 miles / 174 km
from Workington 103 miles / 166 km

You experience the highest point on the route during this section, Black Hill, at 609 metres (1998 feet), just beating Hartside, so again be prepared for the possibility of extreme weather descending on you quickly. If anything the scenery of the North Pennines becomes wilder and grander and continues to be pockmarked by the remains of former mining activity. At Rookhope the off-road route across the moor is the most direct and is superb once you have the initial climb out of the way. The Stanhope option still involves a very steep climb out of the village. After Rookhope you can be secure in the knowledge that you have conquered the really mountainous part of the route and look forward to some downhill cruising to your final destination. The Waskerley Way is an excellent, easy-going and largely well-surfaced dedicated cycle and walking trail that brings you to Consett. It's a superbly relaxing 10 mile cruise downhill to Lydgett's Junction, dropping around 200 metres in the process and taking you over the superb Hownsgill Viaduct. At Lydgett's Junction you must make the choice of Newcastle or Sunderland as your finishing point.

On the old railway bed across Stanhope Common

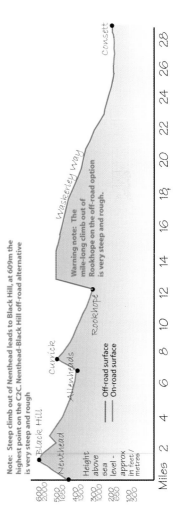

Note: Steep climb out of Nenthead leads to Black Hill, at 609m the highest point on the C2C. Nenthead-Black Hill off-road alternative is very steep and rough

Warning note: The mile-long climb out of Rookhope on the off-road option is very steep and rough.

Off-road surface
On-road surface

Height above sea level - approx in feet / metres

600 / 2000
500 / 1650
400 / 1300
300 / 1000
200 / 650
100 / 300

Black Hill
Nenthead
Allenheads
Currick
Rookhope
Waskerley Way
Consett

Miles 2 4 6 8 10 12 14 16 18 20 22 24 26 28

49

NENTHEAD TO ROOKHOPE Facing the Miners Arms in Nenthead head right and climb steeply up the A689 and take the first left after about 1/2 a mile which will bring you to Black Hill - congratulations you've reached the highest point on the C2C. (For the extremely steep but shorter off-road option to Black Hill face the Miners Arms and go to the right of the former reading room. Bear left in front of Burnside House and as the climb levels out take the next right up a very steep rocky track to emerge at Black Hill). Navigation to Rookhope is now easy; follow signs to Allenheads village where you sweep past the Allenheads Inn and the Hemmel Cafe and across the B6295 to climb over Currick. Head down into valley bottom with Rookhope Burn always on your right, into Rookhope village.

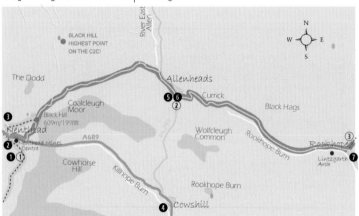

STANHOPE ALTERNATIVE
Simply continue on the road through Rookhope, following the Stanhope road (gated) over the southern end of Stanhope Common. At the A689 follow the cycleway alongside the road and turn left onto the B6278 and after two miles climbing pick up the Waskerley Way on the right.

NAVIGATION TIPS
* The above direction tips will help you navigate but we strongly advise using the official Sustrans map (latest edition) along with this guide.
* See www.c2cplaces2stay.co.uk for online details of accommodation and much more and www.sustrans.org.uk/map for route updates
* The route is signed along much of its length but don't rely purely on signs - check your location against this guide and the Sustrans map.

ROOKHOPE TO CONSETT The main route from
Rookhope is the former railway track across
Stanhope Moor. This involves a steep
climb of just over a mile but the resulting
ride across the moor is a breeze and
has tremendous views. This track
joins the B6278 after 3½ miles
of glorious off-roading.

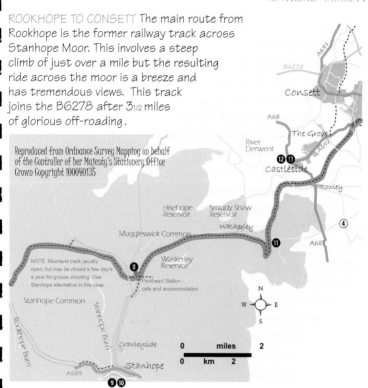

Reproduced from Ordnance Survey Mapping on behalf
of the Controller of her Majesty's Stationery Office
Crown Copyright 100040135

NOTE: Moorland track usually
open, but may be closed a few day's
a year for grouse shooting. Use
Stanhope alternative in this case:

Parkhead Station -
cafe and accommodation

Head over the B6278 and up a track to pass Parkhead Station
B&B and cafe. Bear left to follow the Waskerley Way and into open
moorland again. The Waskerley Reservoir appears down to your
right. Continue across a track crossroads and carry on until you go
through a car park and come to the main road in Rowley. Left onto
main road then very shortly right back onto the Waskerley Way. Pass
over the very impressive Hownsgill Viaduct just before coming to
Lydgett's Junction marked by a large smelt wagon. Carry straight on
to finish at Sunderland or split off left, passing behind the car park,
to finish at Newcastle. Ignore signs for Lanchester Valley.

Hotels and Guesthouses

NENTHEAD

❶ MINERS ARMS Nenthead CA9 3PF (01434) 381427
⌨ www.nenthead.com £35.00 per person per night ⟿1 t/d 1d/tr 🍽 🍽
⏏ drying facilities available ⊡ 🚲 Open all year C2C stamping point
🚶 on the route

❷ CHERRY TREE COTTAGE Nenthead CA9 3PD (01434) 381434
⌨www.cherrytree-cottage.org £25.00 ⟿3d1f1s3triple English Tourism
rated & locally approved 🍽 £5.00 ⏏ ⊡on request 🚲16
✖ Pressure hose Open all year 🚶on route

❸ AVESGARTH 13 Hillersdon Terrace Nenthead CA9 3PG (01434) 382656
⌨ www.avesgarth.mysite.wanadoo-members.co.uk £25.00 ⟿1s1d1t1f 🍽
£3.75 🚲 Open all year 🚶on route

NENTHEAD TO PARKHEAD

❹ LOW CORNRIGGS FARM Cowshill DL13 1AQ (01388) 537600
⌨ www.cornriggsfarm.co.uk £32.00 ◆◆◆◆ 🍽 3-course dinner £17.50 🍽
⏏ ⊡ 🚲 Open all year 🚶4 miles

❺ THE ALLENHEADS INN Allenheads NE47 9HJ (01434) 685200
⌨ www.allenheadsinn.co.uk £35.00 ⟿3d2t4f3s 🍽 - notice day before
⏏ drying room 🚲20 ✖basic tools Open all year 🚶on the route

❻ NEW HOUSES Allenheads NE47 9HX (01434) 685260 ⌨www.
allenheadsC2C.com ⌨zookon@aol.com From £25.00 ⟿ 2t (inc 1 en suite)
1s Locally approved 🍽no but pub nearby 🍽 £4.00 ⏏fire and clothes
horse and tumble dryer ⊡ 🚲 ✖basic tools Open all year
🚶on the route

❼ THE ROOKHOPE INN Rookhope DL13 2BG (01388) 517215
⌨www.rookhope.com From £35.00 (£38.00 Fri,Sat,Sun) ⟿4t1d
🍽 meals every evening and Sunday lunchtimes 🍽 ⏏ ⊡£1.00 🚲10
✖ Bike wash Real ales Live music on Saturday nights Open all year
🚶on the route

❽ PARKHEAD STATION Stanhope Moor DL13 2ES (01388) 526434
⌨ www.parkheadstation.co.uk From £30.00 ⟿2d3f all en-suite ◆◆◆
🍽 evening meals 🍽 ⏏drying room ⊡ 🚲25 with CCTV coverage
✖basic tools and a good range of spares C2C memorabilia available 🚌 by
arrangement Open all year 🚶 on the route at mile 100.

STANHOPE OPTION

❾ BONNY MOORHEN 25 Front Street Stanhope DL13 2TS (01388) 528214
Mobile : 0771 5277300 From £30.00 Discounts for parties of eight or more
and for children under 10 ⚑1f1d2t 🍽 please arrange when booking
🍽£3.00 please arrange when booking ⊺ tumble dryer and radiators ▫ 🚲
Public house with live music Friday and Saturday April to October
Close to shops, takeaways, cafe etc Open all year 🏊 1.3 miles

❿ FOSSIL TREE B&B 2 Market Place Stanhope DL13 2UN 07932 440550 /
(01388) 527851 From £22.00 Locally approved 🍽 £3.50
⊺radiators ▫on request 🚲 Open all year 🏊approx 1 mile

CASTLESIDE

⓫ BEE COTTAGE FARMHOUSE (01207) 508224 Castleside DH8 9HW
🖥 www.beecottage.co.uk £35.00 ⚑2d2t4f ♦♦♦♦ 🍽 three course dinner
including coffee £20.00 🍽 order night before ⊺ laundry / drying room ▫on
request - small charge 🚲30 ✗some basic tools Open all year
🏊 0.2 miles Signed from Waskerley Way

⓬ CASTLENEUK GUEST HOUSE 18 - 20 Front Street Castleside DH8 9AR
(01207) 506634 🖥 www.castleneuk.co.uk £25.00 ⚑2t2d1treble
🍽three course evening meal, fresh home made £12.00 - pre booked please
🍽 pre book please ⊺ ▫free washing and drying - do own ironing 🚲10
✗basic tools 🚗 can be arranged with local firm Bike washing facilities
Free hot / cold drinks on arrival Warm towels in bad weather
Good pub grub 150yards Open all year 🏊one mile

⓭ DENEVIEW 15 Front Street Castleside DH8 9AR (01207) 502925
🖥 www.deneview.co.uk From £25.00 ⚑1t1d English Tourism rated and
locally approved 🍽 pub 50 yards down the road 🍽 ⊺ ▫ 🚲 ✗
Open all year 🏊one mile

Currick 'summit', east of Allenheads, before the descent to Rookhope

Hostels and Campsites

① MILL COTTAGE & ASSAY BUNKHOUSES CA9 3PD Nenthead Mines
Heritage Centre Nenthead (01434) 382726/382037 🖳 www.npht.com
mines@npht.com   £15.00 🛏 18 spaces with linen and towels provided
Locally approved 🍴 self catering facilities 🌡 central heating and radiators
🚲 ⬜ washing machine Open all year 🚶 on route

② THORN GREEN BUNKHOUSE / CAMPGROUND Allenheads NE47 9JQ
(01434) 685234 🖳 hammershields@btopenworld.com £25.00
🛏 2x 6 person dormitories 🍴 🌡 room with radiator ⬜ 🚲 12 (lockable
garage) Area suitable for camping too - £4 per tent plus £2 per person
Shower and toilet facilities for bunkhouses and campers Open all year
🚶 on the route

③ BARRINGTON BUNKHOUSE Rookhope DL13 2BG (01388) 517656
🖳 www.barrington-bunkhouse-rookhope.co.uk B&B £20.00
▲ £14 with breakfast £10 without 🌡 🚲 Open all year 🚶 on route

④ MANOR PARK CARAVAN PARK Broadmeadows Rippon Burn Castleside
DH8 9HD (01207) 501000 ▲30 Toilets Showers 🌡
Open May to September 🚶 2 miles Note: Booking ahead essential and you
must mention you are doing the C2C cycle route.

Out of Nenthead and you are soon riding from Cumbria into
Northumberland

Food and Drink

NENTHEAD **Overwater Lodge Restaurant** is on the route coming into
Nenthead from Garrigill (01434) 381271 www.overwaterlodge.co.uk From
soups, sarnies and light bites to full meals
The Miners Arms (01434) 381427 Offers a full range of snacks and meals
at both lunchtime and evenings. Much used by C2Cers   **Nenthead Mines
Heritage Centre** (01434) 382726/382037 Cafe and picnic area. All on
route **Nenthead Community Shop & Post Office** (01434) 382359
Open 7 days.

ALLENHEADS **Hemmel** The Heritage Centre Allenheads
(01434) 685568   Open all day 9.00 - 5.00 will open by appointment other
hours Can accommodate group bookings for breakfast or other meals All
day breakfasts, some full meals, specials board every day, snacks, cakes
and pastries, vegetarian. Computer facilities available (£1.00 for 15 minutes)
cycle parking outside coffee shop   Shop facilities with off-licence next to
coffee shop on route   **Allenheads Inn** (01434) 685200 Bar lunches and
evening meals daily in this centrally located pub on route

ROOKHOPE **Rookhope Inn** (01388) 517215 Home-cooked food & real ale

PARKHEAD STATION TEAROOMS Stanhope Moor (01388) 526434
 Wholesome, home-made food, snacks, sandwiches and evening meals
Open all year - if there is nobody around please knock or ring!
 by arrangement on the route at mile 100

STANHOPE OPTION

STANHOPE **The Queens Head** (01388) 528160 has home-cooked food and
real ales. on the alternative route   **The Packhorse Inn** (01388) 528407
Bar meals, lunchtime all year and summer evenings. The **Durham Dales
Centre** has tearooms. Open all year (see tourist information on page 57 for
full contact details)

Cottages at Allenheads

Visitor Attractions

Important note on mining landscape: The moorland landscape from the Alston area to the Waskerley Way is littered with remains of old mine workings. These include shafts, adits (horizontal tunnels for drainage or access) and old buildings such as smelt mills. **These are often in a serious state of decay and should not be entered.** As well as obvious sites such as vertical shafts beware of 'hummocky' ground which often contains pit entrances. 'Beehive' cones of stones covered pit entrances and may have partly collapsed. Some of these underground workings were hundreds of feet deep.

NENTHEAD Former mining settlement. Less historic in appearance than Alston it still has features of interest, set amidst wild Pennine scenery. Claims to be England's highest village and has a climate to match (colder than Aberdeen). During winter travellers to Allendale found a journey through the mines easier than going 'over the tops'. Originally a **planned settlement for mine workers** (1825), organised by the same Quaker-based London Lead Company predominant in Alston. Enlightened attitude of the employers meant good working conditions for the time including provision of public baths and pension funds. **Reading room** and impressive **village hall** still remain. Well preserved **Methodist church** reflects former strength of religion. Interesting decorative **fountain** is a memorial to R.W. Bainbridge, superintendent of the mine company.

Nenthead Mines Heritage Centre and Historic Site. Well-preserved site of 200 acres shows numerous remnants of lead and silver mining in its original forbidding landscape. Heritage centre tells the story of the site. Self-guided trails through the site. Cafe. Gift shop and picnic area. You can take a trip underground round some of the old mineworkings. Admission charge. (01434) 382726/382037

Black Hill, at the end of the steep climb out of Nenthead, is the **highest point on the C2C** (609 metres or 1998 feet, so at least your head will be above 2000 feet!). Naturally much photographed.

ALLENHEADS Despite a working history as a lead mining centre this is an estate village that has managed to reinvent itself as a small, popular tourist centre. Unlike lead mining in Nenthead the industry here was controlled by one aristocratic family, the Blackett-Beaumonts. Once a village of nearly 800 people it now has 200 residents. The Allenheads mine closed in 1896, many workers emigrating to the colonies. **Visitor Centre** explores the history of the local lead mines and what has happened here since the last lead mine closed. The **Blacksmiths Shop and Engine House** is another reminder of the village's past.

ROOKHOPE Approaching Rookhope is a working fluospar mine and further down the valley is the **Lintzgarth Arch**, only remains of a bridge that once carried a 2 mile long horizontal flue across the valley. This was cleaned by child labour to recoup lead deposits accumulated as smelting fumes were carried away up the hillside. An old smelt mill is in the centre. Main route over Stanhope Moor follows the line of an old railway line, once the **highest standard gauge route in Britain**, that carried mineral ore to Consett, continuing to the latter as the Waskerley Way.

STANHOPE OPTION Self-proclaimed capital of Weardale and attractive market town. **Durham Dales Centre** is set in the lovely Castle Gardens, the castle really being an elaborate 18th century folly.

THE WASKERLEY WAY boasts plenty of flora and fauna and the spectacular heights of the **Hownsgill Viaduct**.

Open moorland, easy gradients, solitude - it's the Waskerley Way

Bike Shops and Other Facilities

1. MR. MARK FEARN Nenthead (01434) 382194 Mob. 0777 6098915
💻 www.markfearn.co.uk Blacksmith with a modest stock of spares who can repair most bikes. When possible operates a rider / bike recovery service.

2. NORTH PENNINE CYCLES Nenthead CA9 3PS (01434) 381324

3. PARKHEAD STATION Stanhope Moor DL13 2ES (01388) 526434
🔧 basic tools and a good range of spares available at this tearooms/B&B.
🚌 by arrangement Open all year - if there is nobody around please knock!
🚲 on the route at mile 100

Tourist Information

STANHOPE TOURIST INFORMATION Castle Gardens Stanhope DL13 2FJ
(01388) 527650 💻 www.durhamdalescentre.co.uk

The Allenheads Inn is a well-known spot for C2Cers to stop for a bite or to bed down for the night

C2C route at Lintzgarth Arch near Rookhope

5A Consett - Sunderland

Route Info

24 miles / 37km
Off - road - virtually all off-road with
occasional road section
Accumulated distance from
Whitehaven 133 miles / 214 km
from
Workington 127 miles / 204 km

Penshaw Monument from the Wear

For most of the way the Consett and
Sunderland railway path is flat and easy
to follow. The tendency is to speed on
but doing this you can easily miss the
many attractions close to the route such
as Beamish Museum. Unfortunately
the Consett - Sunderland railway path
has more access barriers than the
Newcastle option along the Derwent
Walk. The railpath is a mix of cinder track
and tarmac and generally gets better
and better towards Sunderland before
a spectacular finish down lovely wide,
red tarmac past the Stadium of Light to
Roker. Once, real difficulties in navigation
lay in negotiating Sunderland city
centre but a 'north bank' route has been
introduced and is a great improvement
in terms of track condition and ease
of navigation. There are also plenty of
mileposts to help navigation. Physically
this is the easiest section of the whole
route. The landscape presents a strong
contrast; the Wear Valley is delightfully
green and wooded in places, dotted with
specially commissioned sculptures and
other monuments, whilst Sunderland
presents a grand spectacle of post-
industrial decay that is steadily and
thoughtfully being regenerated, together
with many interesting museums and
buildings.

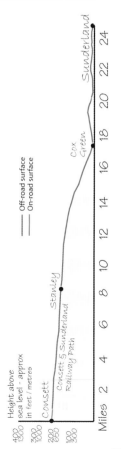

CONSETT TO CHESTER LE STREET

Lydgetts Junction is marked by the unmistakable bulk of the Smelt Wagon. Those heading directly for Newcastle / Tynemouth (NCN 14) should bear left whilst those who want Sunderland (NCN 72) and / or Consett centre go straight on (ignore a right to Lanchester and Durham on NCN14). Just after Terris Novalis sculpture you can choose the Consett centre option to the left (see map on page 72) or carry straight on to parallel the south side of the A69 on shared use pathway. Both options meet again to the south-east of Sunderland and join the Consett & Sunderland railway path. It is now mainly a matter of following the railpath. Cross the road in Leadgate centre and pick up the railpath again. You approach Annfield Plain past a pond on the left then jink left then right over a road and on to cross the A693 on a bridge. Head down Dodds Terrace then St Aidans Terrace to main road in Annfield Plain. Straight across back onto railpath.

Reproduced from Ordnance Survey Mapping on behalf of the Controller of her Majesty's Stationery Office
Crown Copyright 100040135

As you cruise down the railpath keep a track of where you are, especially if you want to stop off at such places as Beamish (railpath near here features metal cow sculptures). You pass north of Stanley centre on this traffic-free trail, then through open country on your approach to Chester-Le-Street, all the while passing under and over numerous roads. The classical looking Penshaw monument is clearly visible on this section and confirms your general direction.

NAVIGATION TIPS

* The above direction tips will help you navigate but we strongly advise using the official Sustrans map (latest edition) along with this guide.
* See www.c2cplaces2stay.co.uk for online details of accommodation and much more and www.sustrans.org.uk/map for route updates
* The route is signed along much of its length but don't rely purely on signs · check your location against this guide and the Sustrans map.

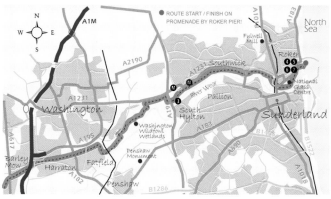

CHESTER LE STREET TO SUNDERLAND

Pass over the A167 and under A1(M), passing Chester-Le-street to the south then Washington to the north. Careful navigation required at Fatfield; pass over Newman Lane and bear right down tree-lined track by a railway on the left. Bear left to pass under railway bridge into James Steel Park and swing right to descend steeply to River Wear. By green footbridge climb away from river onto a series of paths. Turn right parallel to a road then dip and climb past Washington Wildfowl Wetlands. Bear left at tarmac road then right in about 150m to come alongside A1231 on your left. This track swings right and takes you under the A19 to a steep descent to the Shipwrights Hotel. See detailed A to Z maps for Sunderland navigation.

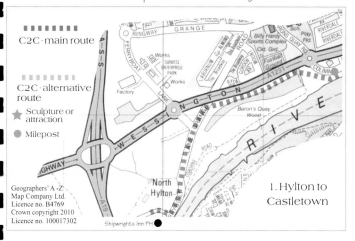

■■■■■■■■
C2C·main route

■■■■■■■■
C2C·alternative route

★ Sculpture or attraction

● Milepost

Geographers' A -Z
Map Company Ltd.
Licence no. B4769
Crown copyright 2010
Licence no. 100017302

1. Hylton to Castletown

61

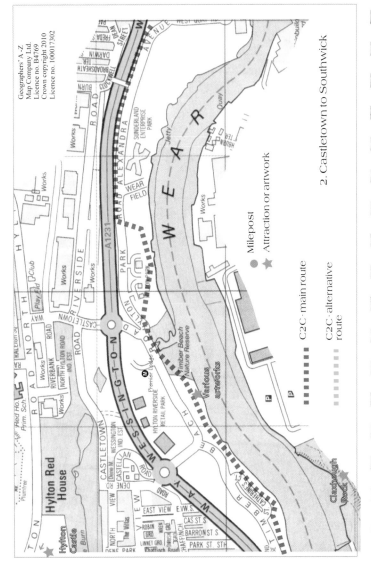

Geographers' A-Z
Map Company Ltd.
Licence no. B4769
Crown copyright 2010
Licence no. 100017302

2. Castletown to Southwick

● Milepost

★ Attraction or artwork

▪▪▪ C2C - main route

▫▫▫ C2C - alternative route

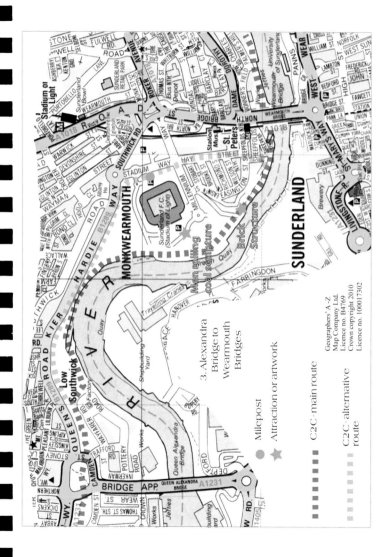

3. Alexandra Bridge to Wearmouth Bridges

● Milepost

★ Attraction or artwork

▪ C2C · main route

▪ C2C · alternative route

Geographers' A-Z
Map Company Ltd.
Licence no. B4769
Crown copyright 2010
Licence no. 100017302

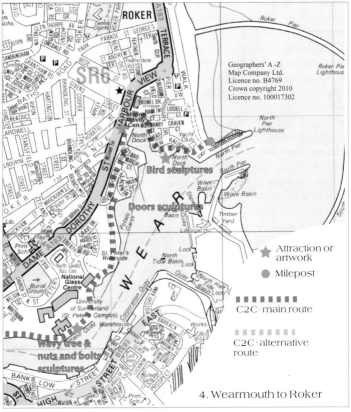

Geographers' A -Z
Map Company Ltd.
Licence no. B4769
Crown copyright 2010
Licence no. 100017302

★ Attraction or artwork

● Milepost

■■■■■■■■
C2C · main route

■■■■■■■■
C2C · alternative route

4. Wearmouth to Roker

A lovely view unfolds as you sweep round the corner towards the Wearmouth Bridges

Hotels and Guesthouses

CONSETT TO SUNDERLAND

❶ BEAMISH MARY INN No Place Beamish DH9 0AQ (0191) 3700237 / 07946 730048 🖥 www.beamishmaryinn.co.uk Prices from £35.00 ♦♦♦ 🍴 🍴 🚲
✗ Live entertainment   Open all year 🎒800 yards (behind Beamish Museum)

❷ MALLING HOUSE 1 Oakdale Terrace Newfield Chester-Le-Street DH2 2SU
(0191) 3702571 🖥 mallinghouse1@hotmail.co.uk £35.00 ♦♦♦
🍴 no but can offer advice on local eateries Microwave available for own
food   🍴 🌂 ⬜ wet clothes washed and dried, tumble dryer available   🚲6
🚃 where possible   Open all year   🎒0.25 miles

SUNDERLAND

❸ SHIPWRIGHTS HOTEL Ferryboat Lane North Hylton SR5 3HW
(0191) 5495139 £26.00 🎒 on route

❹ ANCHOR LODGE 16 Roker Terrace Roker Sunderland SR6 9NB
(0191) 5674154 Mobile 07973 318210 🖥www.anchorlodgeuk.co.uk
£22.00 - £25.00 ♦♦♦ 🍴 🌂boiler house with lines ⬜can be arranged
🚲 ✗ Pressure washer Open 365 days a year 🎒100 yards

❺ ASHBORNE GUEST HOUSE 7 St. George's Terrace Sunderland SR6 9LX
(0191) 5653997 🖥www.ashborne-guesthouse.co.uk From £23.00
⤴ 4t2d2f ♦♦♦ 🍴 🌂 🚲 ✗basic tools Open all year 🎒 on route

❻ BELMONT GUEST HOUSE 8 St. George's Terrace Roker Sunderland SR6 9LX
(0191) 5672438 Mobile 078 3378 7481 🖥 www.belmontguesthouse.com
£20.00 - £22.00 ♦♦♦ 🍴no but several restaurants within walking distance
🍴charge 🌂tumble dry £2.00 ⬜ £2.00 a load 🚲
Open all days 🎒two minutes walk from eastern end of route

❼ THE CHAISE GUEST HOUSE 5 Roker Terrace Roker Sunderland SR6 9NB
(0191) 5659218 🖥www.thechaiseguesthouse.com Prices from £18.50 ⤴d/t/
f/s ♦♦♦ 🍴 🍴 evening meals and packed lunches 🌂 ⬜ 🚲
Open all year round 🎒near route

Ⓜ There are 2 motel style operations very near the route on this section:
PREMIER INN, Wessington Way, Castletown SR5 3HR 0871 5279058
🎒200 yards
PREMIER INN, Timber Beach Road, Castletown SR5 3XG 0871 5279056
🎒100 yards

Hostels and Campsites

① CONSETT YMCA Parliament Street Consett DH8 5DH (01207) 502680
🖥www.consettymca.org £12.50per person plus £5 for breakfast if required -
minimum booking 6 people unless there are other bookings for the same date
🛏9f 🍽 evening meal 🍽 request night before 🌡radiators and drying room
🚲 15 - 20   Open all year   🚶200 metres

② BOBBY SHAFTO CARAVAN PARK Cranberry Plantation Beamish
Stanley DH9 0RY (0191) 370 1776   🖥www.bobbyshaftocaravanpark.co.uk
▲20 ★★★ Open 1st March to 31st October 🚶1 mile

Food and Drink

CONSETT centre has a range of eateries. The oldest pub in town, **The Grey
Horse**, (01207) 502585 is also a brewery selling its own ales (even a C2C ale!)
and snacks Open daily from noon 🚶0.25 miles from the route. Cycle locking
points outside. Consett town centre.

JOLLY DROVERS PUB (01207) 503994 Full bar menu 🚶On the route just
after Leadgate (the C2C emerges in the car park then crosses the main road
roundabout to continue on the railpath)

BEAMISH **Beamish Mary Inn** No Place Beamish (0191) 3700237
🖥ianhope@hotmail.com Food - lunchtimes and evenings. Real ales. 1920s
and 1930s decor Open all year 🚶800 yards **Shepherd and Shepherdess
Pub** (0191) 3700349 Has food on offer all day every day. Only about 300m
north of the route. **Beamish Museum** (0191) 3704000 has a choice of eateries - Dainty Dinah Tea Rooms, Sun Inn public house (period recreation pub),
Coffee Shop, Pitman's Pantry and The Cart Shed. At least one is open during
museum opening hours. 🚶Less than 0.5 miles

SHIPWRIGHTS HOTEL (0191) 5495139 A range of ales and meals. Right next
to the C2C as you come into North Hylton under the A19.

WASHINGTON WILDFOWL WETLANDS CENTRE (0191) 4165454
Has a cafe and picnic area. Cycle rack parking. Open daily throughout the year.
🚶Next to route.

SUNDERLAND Of course, the town centre has a great choice of venues but to
splash out and celebrate the end of your journey why not try **Throwingstones**
at the National Glass Centre on Liberty Way (0191) 5653939; well-known and
classy, its offerings range from snacks to seafood bisque. 🚶Next to route. The
Marina Activity Centre is a stamping point and effective end point for many
C2Cers; get a coffee, a bite and even take a shower then dry off with one of
their C2C towels! (0191) 5144721

Note that the Motel style accommodation listed on page 65 has restaurant
services offering food throughout the day.

Visitor Attractions

TERRIS NOVALIS There are many specially commissioned sculptures along the C2C route but this is one of the most outstanding. 20 foot high stainless steel surveying instruments symbolise the regeneration of Consett after the closure of the massive steel works that was the heart of the area.

BEAMISH AND AROUND **Beamish Open Air Museum** (0191) 3704000 is one of the North's premier museums. Unique full-scale recreation of the past industrial and agricultural life of the North-East. Visit a drift mine, pit cottages, a 19th century manor farm or hop on a tram, plus lots more attractions at this huge site in Beamish Burn. Also houses a tourist information centre. Admission fee. ⛵Less than 0.5 miles north of the route. **Causey Arch**, centrepiece of a beautiful picnic site, is one of the main features of the **Tanfield Railway** (🖥 www.tanfield-railway.co.uk) and is the oldest surviving single-arch railway bridge in the world. The railway was opened in 1725 and used horses to haul small coal wagons along wooden tracks. It is now a steam railway run by volunteers. Open to the public on selected days - 0845 4634938 for details ⛵East Tanfield station is just under a mile from the route

CHESTER LE STREET Few physical remains left of Roman influence in its name but impressive spire on church and effigies of the Lumley family inside. **Ankers House Museum** (0191) 3883295 Church Chare, town centre. See how an Anchorite lived, walled up for life to pray. Free admission. April-Oct, Mon-Sat and bank hols.

WASHINGTON was created as a new town in 1967, designed to attract industry and jobs to a declining area. Divided into self-contained village type settlements and with planned segregation of cars and pedestrians.
'F' Pit Mining Museum, Albany Way. Winding house and engine on display. **Arts Centre Washington**, Fatfield, houses exhibitions and performances.
James Steel Park surrounds the Wear between Fatfield and Barmston. Houses **Victoria Viaduct** (completed on Victoria's coronation day, 28th June, 1838) and **Worm Hill** of Lambton Worm fame. The 'Worm' was a mythical dragon that brought about a family curse when slain. **The Penshaw Monument** is based on the Temple of Hephaestus in Athens. A memorial to 'Radical Jack' Lambton, 1st Earl of Durham, it was built in 1844 from public subscription. Good views of it from James Steel Park and around Cox Green.

Terris Novalis - just south of Consett on the route to Sunderland.

Washington Wildfowl Trust (0191) 4165454 District 15
💻 www.wwt.org.uk/centre/123/washington.html Important and extensive site for wildlife, especially winter wildfowl. **Washington Old Hall** (0191) 4166879 for opening details The Avenue, District 4, Washington Village. A National Trust property incorporating the remains of the home of George Washington's ancestors, within a 17th century manor house. Tea room.

SUNDERLAND Once one of the world's greatest shipbuilding towns. The shipbuilding area can still be seen from Wearmouth Bridge. One of England's newest cities and the centre of much regeneration, e.g. St. Peter's Riverside - this area houses the **National Glass Centre** (0191) 5155555 which has galleries, a shop and free entry. Wearmouth also houses the **Stadium of Light** football ground and the C2C passes a **new marina** development. **Wearmouth Bridge** road bridge dwarfs the railway bridge next to it. Built 1927-8, the parapet has a medallion showing the 1796 bridge it replaced. A technological wonder of its day. **North East Aircraft Museum** (0191) 5190662, 1.5 miles north of the C2C in North Hylton, has aircraft and military vehicles. **St. Andrew's Church**, Roker is regarded as the 'cathedral' of William Morris' Arts and Craft Movement. Phone for opening times (0191) 5160135

Fulwell Mill North-west of Roker. Most complete windmill in the north east and fully restored. **Hylton Castle** (0191) 5367776 15th century keep-gatehouse still survives. West side has heavy battlements. Museum. Free admission to view exterior only. **St.Peters Church** One of Northumbria's oldest churches with Saxon wall and tower. Home of the Venerable Bede, 'Father of English History'. Much of it reconstructed in Victorian times. Phone for opening times (0191) 5160135 **Monkwearmouth Station Museum**. (0191) 5677075 Housed in train station with grand classical facade. Railway museum with a genuine 19th century atmosphere. Victorian booking office, Victorian and Edwardian cycle displays and lots more Free admission. Third of a mile north of Wearmouth Bridge **Sunderland Museum & Winter Gardens** (0191) 5532323, gives you the lowdown on the town's history and has a fine art gallery whilst the Winter Gardens have over 1,500 plants and flowers. **Northern Gallery for Contemporary Art** (0191) 5618407 The north-east's premier collection of contemporary art. **Sunderland Volunteer Life Brigade Museum**. Near the end of the C2C. Volunteers preceded the RNLI as the main body responsible on this stretch of coast for ship rescue. Brigade now separated from the coastguard service and acts as auxiliary service for coastal services and cliff rescue. Still a working brigade; only one of 3 left out of an original 40. Free entry. Sunday 12-6 and some evenings. (0191) 5292651

Famous road and rail bridges over the River Wear - a major landmark as you head towards Sunderland

Bike Shops

MO - TECH CYCLES 62 Medomsley Road Consett DH8 5HP
(01207) 591912 ⌨www.mo-tech-bikes.co.uk Spares & repairs. 🚲0.1 mile from
town centre route

CESTRIA CYCLES 11 Ashfield Terrace Chester le Street DH3 3PD
(0191) 3887535 ⌨www.cestriacycles.co.uk Spares & repairs 🚲1.2 miles

HOUGHTON CYCLES 3 West View Concord Washington NE37 2DT
(0191) 4169906 Spares & repairs If busy ring Houghton le Spring shop on
(0191) 5844465   🚲1.9 miles

CYCLE WORLD 222 High Street West Sunderland SR1 1TZ (0191) 5658188
or 5141974 ⌨www.cycleworldshop.co.uk Spares & repairs 🚲0.25 miles

PETER DARKE CYCLES 1&2 John St Sunderland SR1 1DX (0191) 5108155
⌨www.peterdarkecycles.com Cycle hire including tandems Spares & repairs
Call-out within 5 - 10 miles
🚲0.3 miles

HALFORDS SUPERSTORE Trimdon Street Sunderland SR4 6DW
(0191) 5140843 Spares & repairs 🚲0.75 miles

KELLY'S CYCLES 148 Chester Road Sunderland SR4 7EY (0191) 5142265
Spares & repairs 🚲1 mile

Tourist Information

NORTH OF ENGLAND OPEN AIR MUSEUM TIC, Beamish DH9 0RG
(0191) 3704000 ⌨ www.beamish.org.uk

SUNDERLAND TOURIST INFORMATION 50 Fawcett Street SR1 1RF
(0191) 5532000 ⌨www.sunderland.gov.uk

Steel cows made of recycled metal grace (and graze) the side
of the Consett to Sunderland railpath near Beamish

The Sunderland skyline as seen from the C2C

Traffic free trail as you head south of Consett towards Sunderland

71

5B Consett - Tynemouth

Route Info

28 miles / 45 km   **Off - road - virtually all off-road with occasional road section**

Accumulated distance from Whitehaven 137 miles / 220 km
from Workington 131 miles / 211 km

Gentle downhill pedalling, with lengthy sections on specially surfaced off-road track on various designated trails. The Derwent Walk is followed for much of its length from Consett to Swalwell and is a pleasure to ride with very few restrictive access barriers. The route along the Tyne's north bank (Hadrian's Way) is greatly improved from the original C2C route with a lot of new traffic-free trail laid. The alternative option along the Tyne's southern bank has been much improved and is an interesting option, though not as spectacular as Hadrian's Way along the northern bank.

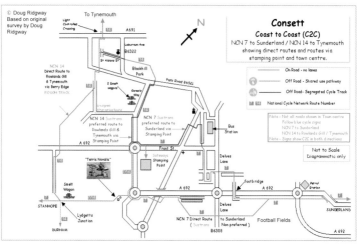

CONSETT TO THE TYNE (Berry Edge option - for Consett centre option see map opposite) At Lydgetts Junction turn left just before smelt wagon onto track behind car park. Continue for about 500 yards to cross over A692 and climb the rocky track and continue over the open area of Berry Edge (follow yellow squares / Derwent Walk signs). Jink right - left to cross over Park Road and pass St Aidans Street on the right (link to Consett centre down here via pretty Blackhill Park). Across the A691 you are firmly on the Derwent Walk.

Pass over a series of viaducts on the Derwent Walk and come to a minor road in Rowlands Gill. Right then left onto B6314. Route follows cycle path on opposite side of B6314. Right goes to Gibside. Continue on cycle path to A694 and continue right on cycle path. Still in Rowlands Gill look for the right turn back onto the Derwent Walk. Just over Nine Arches Viaduct the route leaves the Derwent Walk to follow the north bank of the Derwent, through Derwenthaugh Park. Don't miss the left turn over the stone bridge across the Derwent. Follow the traffic-free route north of the Derwent, under several roads, to arrive at the railway bridge and pass under it for the north bank route (NCN72); if you want the south bank route (NCN14) head over the footbridge next to the railway to cross the Derwent. Now use the A to Z street maps on pages 75 to 82.

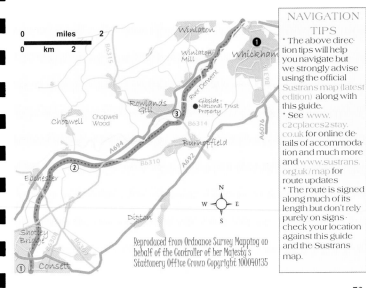

NAVIGATION TIPS

* The above direction tips will help you navigate but we strongly advise using the official Sustrans map (latest edition) along with this guide.
* See www.c2cplaces2stay.co.uk for online details of accommodation and much more and www.sustrans.org.uk/map for route updates
* The route is signed along much of its length but don't rely purely on signs - check your location against this guide and the Sustrans map.

Reproduced from Ordnance Survey Mapping on behalf of the Controller of her Majesty's Stationery Office Crown Copyright 100040135

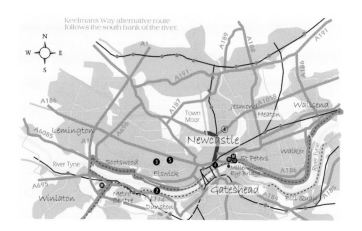

Maps reproduced from Ordnance Survey Mapping on behalf of the Controller of her Majesty's Stationery Office Crown Copyright 100040135

NEWCASTLE STREET MAPPING

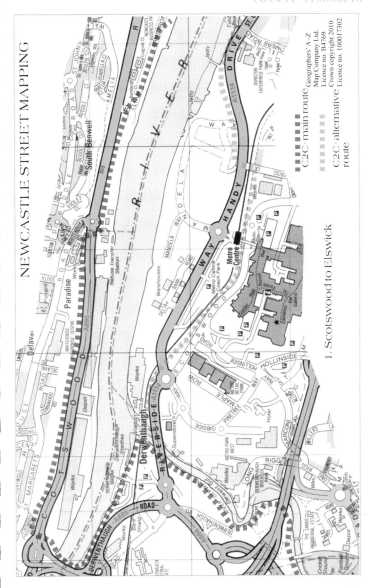

C2C - main route
C2C - alternative route

Geographers' A-Z
Map Company Ltd.
Licence no. B4769
Crown copyright 2010
Licence no. 100017302

1. Scotswood to Elswick

75

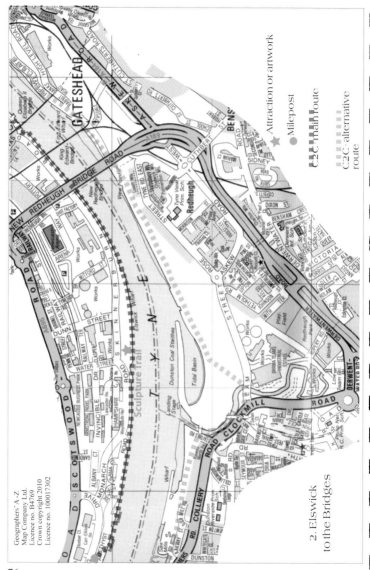

Attraction or artwork
Milepost
C2C main route
C2C alternative route

2. Elswick to the Bridges

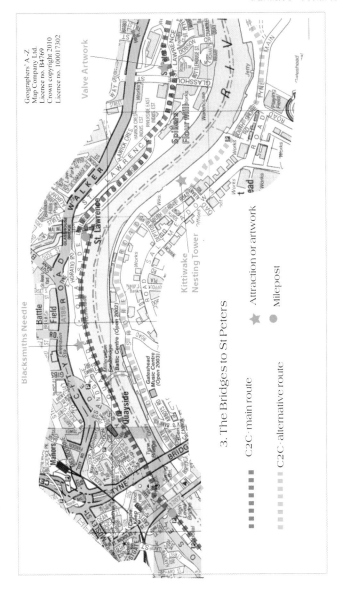

Geographers' A-Z
Map Company Ltd.
Licence no. B4769
Crown copyright 2010
Licence no. 100017302

Valve Artwork

Spillers Flour Mill

Blacksmiths Needle

Kittiwake
Nesting Tower

3. The Bridges to St Peters

★ Attraction or artwork

● Milepost

▪▪▪▪▪ C2C - main route

▪▪▪▪▪ C2C - alternative route

77

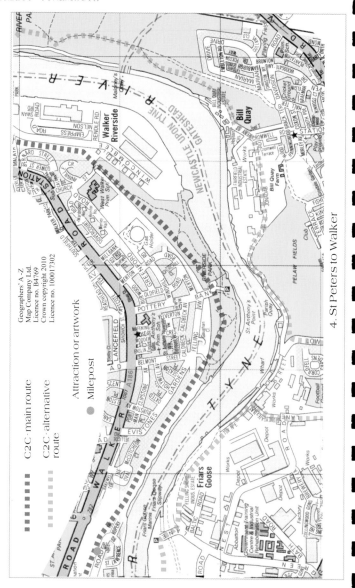

Geographers' A-Z
Map Company Ltd.
Licence no. B4769
Crown copyright 2010
Licence no. 100017302

● Attraction or artwork
● Milepost

▬▬▬ C2C - main route

▬▬▬ C2C - alternative
route

4. St Peters to Walker

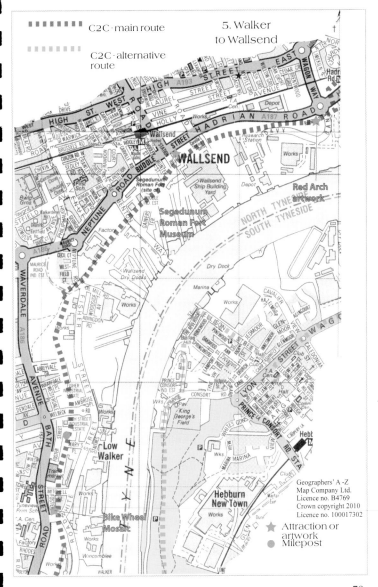

■■■■■■■ C2C · main route

■■■■■■ C2C · alternative route

5. Walker to Wallsend

Red Arch artwork

Segedunum Roman Fort Museum

Bike Wheel Mosaic

Geographers' A -Z
Map Company Ltd.
Licence no. B4769
Crown copyright 2010
Licence no. 100017302

★ Attraction or artwork
● Milepost

79

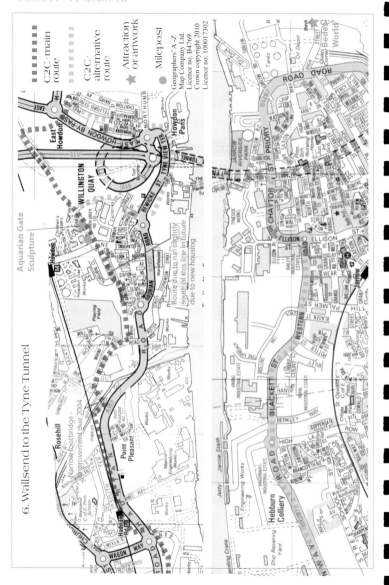

6. Wallsend to the Tyne Tunnel

Aquarian Gate Sculpture

Route due to run slightly south of this line in future due to new housing

C2C - main route
C2C - alternative route
★ Attraction or artwork
● Milepost

Geographers' A-Z
Map Company Ltd.
Licence no. B4769
Crown copyright 2010
Licence no. 100017302

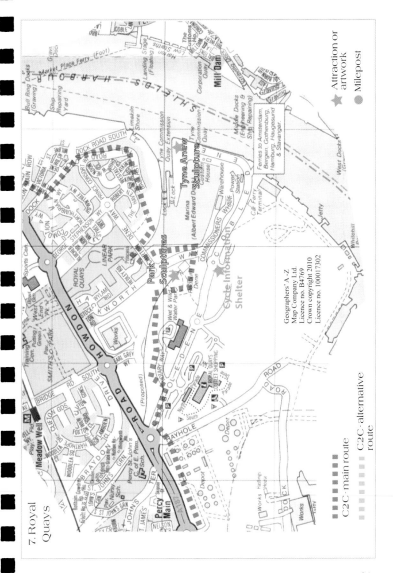

7. Royal Quays

Attraction or artwork

Milepost

Geographers' A-Z.
Map Company Ltd.
Licence no. B4769
Crown copyright 2010
Licence no. 100017302

C2C: main route

C2C: alternative route

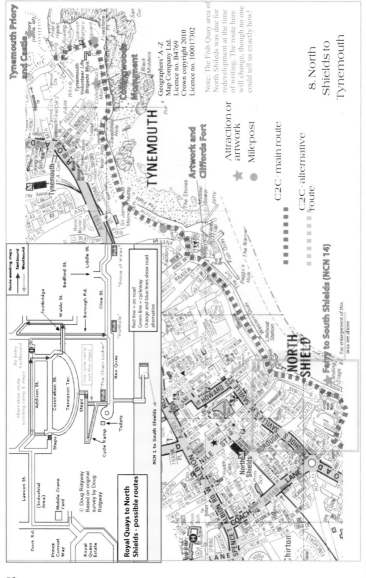

Tynemouth Priory and Castle

Collingwood Monument

Geographers' A-Z
Map Company Ltd.
Licence no. B4769
Crown copyright 2010
Licence no. 100017302

Note: The Fish Quay area of North Shields was due for redevelopment at the time of writing. The route here will change, though no one could tell us exactly how!

8. North Shields to Tynemouth

TYNEMOUTH

⭐ Attraction or artwork

● Milepost

Artwork and Cliffords Fort

▬▬▬ C2C - main route

▬▬▬ C2C - alternative route

Ferry to South Shields (NCN 14)

For enlargement of this area see above

NORTH SHIELDS

Royal Quays to North Shields - possible routes

Red line = on road
Green line = cycleway
Orange and blue lines show road alternative

© Doug Ridgway
Based on original survey by Doug Ridgway

Dock Rd.
Prince Consort Way
Royal Quays Estate

Lawson St.
(Industrial Area)
Mobile Crane Yard

Route avoiding steps
→ Eastbound
→ Westbound

No Entry Eastbound

alternative route avoiding ramp & steps

Footbridge

Addison St.
Coronation St.
Tennyson Ter.

Steps
Steps
Steps
Use cycle ramp - not the steps

Waldo St.
Bedford St.
Borough Rd.
Clive St.
Liddle St.

"Prince of Wales"
Pub

Pub "Porthole"

New Quay

Pub "The Chain Locker"

Cycle Ramp
Toilets

NCN 1 to South Shields

82

Hotels and Guesthouses

CONSETT TO NEWCASTLE

❶ GIBSIDE HOTEL Front Street Whickham NE16 4JG (0191) 488 9292
🖳 www.gibside-hotel.co.uk reception@gibside-hotel.co.uk
From £37.50 room only ⤻ all t/d but can accommodate singles ★★★
🍽 breakfast, bar snacks and a la carte lunch and evening - sandwiches
available all day 🍽 ⌐ ⊡ ⤌ ✗ basic tools Open all year
🛏approximately 1 mile

NEWCASTLE

❷ ROWERS HOTEL St Omers Road Dunston NE11 9EJ (0191) 460 6481
£27.50 ⤻4s4d2t ♦♦♦♦ 🍽 Fully licensed restaurant 🍽 order on check-in -
24hours notice preferred ⌐ ⊡ ⤌ ✗basic tools Hose available for washing
bikes Open all year 🛏on the south bank alternative route (Keelman's Way) at
Dunston, 100 yards from the riverside

❸ CLIFTON HOUSE HOTEL 46 Clifton Road off Grainger Park Road
Newcastle upon Tyne NE4 6XH (0191) 2730407 🖳 www.cliftonhousehotel.com
From £32.50 ⤻1s en suite 4t/d en suite 2s standard ♦♦♦ 🍽£5.00 ⌐ ⊡
⤌ ✗ Open all year 🛏1 mile

❹ WATERSIDE HOTEL 48-52 Sandhill Newcastle upon Tyne NE1 3JF
(0191) 2300111 🖳 www.watersidehotel.com enquiries@watersidehotel.com
£42.50 ⤻36 rooms ★★★ ⌐ ⊡ ⤌ Open all year 🛏on the route

❺ BENTLEYS HOTEL 427 Westgate Road Newcastle upon Tyne NE4 8RL
(0191) 2733497 🖳 www.bentleyshotelandcoffeeshop.co.uk From £20
Coffee shop on premises, open daily until 5pm ⤻2s2t1d ♦♦ ⤌5 Open
all year except 2 weeks around Xmas 🛏approx 1 mile

The Gibside estate lies near the traffic-free Derwent
Walk (part of the C2C), near Rowland's Gill

83

🅜(🅜=motels) PREMIER INN Derwent Haugh Road Swalwell NE16 3BL
0871 5278792 🚶0.5 miles
PREMIER INN Quayside Lombard St Newcastle NE1 3AE 0870 9906530
🚶on route
PREMIER INN City Road Quayside Newcastle NE1 2AN 0871 5278800
🚶0.2 miles
TRAVELODGE Forster Street Newcastle NE1 2NH 0871 9846164
🚶100 yards

TYNEMOUTH

❻ MARTINEAU GUEST HOUSE 57 Front Street Tynemouth NE30 4BX
(0191) 2579038   mobile 07932 784008 🖳 www.martineau-house.co.uk
£47.50 🛏 1t2d (singles accommodated)   ♦♦♦♦   🍽 no but plenty of
restaurants within 200 yards 🍽 ⊺ 🚴   ✗ no but cycle shop nearby
Open all year 🚶 quarter of a mile Some rooms have a minimum 2 night
booking for weekends

❼ SIXTY ONE 61 Front Street Tynemouth NE30 4BT (0191) 2573687
🖳 www.no61.co.uk From £30.00 🛏3d2t/s1f all en suite ♦♦♦♦ 🍽 notice needed
⊺ 🚴 No smoking throughout Open all year   🚶quarter of a mile

Hostels and Campsites

① CONSETT YMCA Parliament Street Consett DH8 5DH (01207) 502680
🖳 www.consettymca.org £12.50per person plus £5 for breakfast if required -
minimum booking 6 people unless there are other bookings for the same date
🛏9f 🍽 evening meal 🍽 request night before ⊺radiators and drying room
🚴 15 - 20 Open all year 🚶200 metres

② BYRESIDE CARAVAN SITE Hamsterley NE17 7RT (01207) 560280
🖳 www.byresidecaravansite.co.uk ⛺8 ★★★★   Toilets and showers etc.
Open all year 🚶adjacent to route

③ DERWENT CARAVAN PARK Rowlands Gill NE39 1LG (01207) 543383
£10.00 (two person tent) Locally approved ⛺ Toilets etc. ⊺ electric clothes
dryer ⊡ 🚴secure lock rings Open 1st March until 31st October
🚶200 metres

④ NEWCASTLE YOUTH HOSTEL 107 Jesmond Road Newcastle upon
Tyne NE2 1NJ 0845 3719335 🖳www.yha.org.uk   newcastle@yha.org.
uk   £16.40 adult £12.50 u18 🛏 50 places in two to eight bedded rooms
★ ★   🍽breakfast and evening meals available - also self catering kitchen 🍽
🚴 Open all year except Christmas 🚶approx 0.5 miles

Food and Drink

CROWN AND CROSSED SWORDS HOTEL Shotley Bridge (01207) 502006
Traditional food served - lunch and dinner
Accommodation available   🚲   🚶2 miles

THE DERWENT WALK INN Ebchester (01207) 560347 Quality bar food 🚲
cycle rack with good vision from inside building 🚶on the route at Ebchester

ROWLANDS GILL **Tea for Two** on Station Road (01207) 542818.
🚶Just off the route at Rowlands Gill

GIBSIDE POTTING SHED TEAROOM & RENWICK'S COFFEE SHOP
(01207) 541828 Open daily See visitor attractions for details of this National
Trust property.

RUN OF THE MILL Winlaton Mill (0191) 4142731 Bar menu and a la carte
daily 🚶Near the route as you pass along the Derwent Walk path at Winlaton
Mill

NEWCASTLE CENTRE, less than a mile north of the route at the Swing
Bridge, has everything from American to Thai restaurants, including Japanese
and Mongolian. The city has a particularly strong tradition of Italian food.
🖥 www.newcastle.gov.uk has a good listing of restaurants in the city. There
is a good selection of places to stop off if just passing through along the river.
The Caffe Vivo on Broad Chare is just north of the route before the Gateshead
Millennium Bridge at the Live Theatre. Imaginative menu of lunches and
snacks.

SEGEDUNUM ROMAN FORT (0191) 2369347 has a cafe, open daily next to
the museum. Lock your bikes outside where there is CCTV.

SOUTH BANK ROUTE
BALTIC CENTRE FOR CONTEMPORARY ART The **Baltic Cafe Bar** (0191)
4404948 has morning pastries, lunchtime sandwiches and afternoon tea and
cakes. Open daily till 5.30. For a true blow-out try the full a la carte meals from
Six, the rooftop restaurant. Lunches and evenings.

JARROW HALL CAFE (0191) 4892106 A good range of snacks and meals in
what is Bede's World (see visitor attractions) museum cafe 🚶Less than a mile
to the east of the route at the Tyne Tunnel. If you want to continue on the south
bank on NCN14 to the South Shields-North Shields ferry crossing then this is
bang on your route.

TYNEMOUTH has plenty on offer to eat and drink. Front Street has a good
clutch of eateries. **Porters Coffee House** at Tynemouth Metro station is also a
C2C stamping point.

Note that the Motel style accommodation listed on page 84 has restaurant
services offering food throughout the day.

Visitor Attractions

CONSETT TO THE TYNE Approaching Consett the rough area of wasteland is **Berry Edge**, 700 acre site of the former Consett steelworks, closed in 1980. Much of the subsequent section follows the lovely **Derwent Walk Path**, based on the line of the 19th century Derwent Valley Railway. It crosses spectacular viaducts such as Pontburn, Fogoesburn and Nine Arches. Now tree-clad along much of its length and housing wildlife such as woodpeckers and sparrowhawks. The largest area of ancient woodland is around Thornley Woodland Centre. Derwent Walk Country Park surrounding the path is one of the largest in northern England. **Shotley Bridge** Home of 17th century swordmakers, still houses reminders of its spa town origins, such as the Cutlers Hall. **Ebchester** Site of the Roman fort Vindamora. Small museum at Mains Farm includes hypocaust (heated space under the floor of a Roman house). The site was once on Dere Street, the Roman road bringing supplies north to the Firth of Forth. Opposite church in Ebchester village. Viewed by appointment on (01207) 562180.

Rowlands Gill, developed as a mining settlement, is now a pleasant suburb with numerous shops and pub. **Gibside** Beautiful 18th century landscaped grounds including Old Hall, extraordinary Palladian Chapel, Orangery, British Liberty statue and Banqueting Hall. Allow a couple of hours to stroll round grounds. Coal-owner George Bowes was responsible for most of the magnificent relandscaping and is buried in the chapel crypt. National Trust. Admission charge. Opening details ring (01207) 541820. A real 'must'.

NEWCASTLE UPON TYNE Most famous for **heavy industry and coal**. Previously one of the largest ship building and repair centres in the world. The cranes and derricks around Walker Riverside are still an impressive spectacle. Once had one of the most **elegant townscapes** in the country and countless interesting buildings and monuments remain despite crass 60s and 70s modernisation. **Grey St**. has been described as one of the most elegant streets in Europe. Also famous for bridges, most notably the **Gateshead Millennium Bridge**. The world's only tilting bridge, allowing shipping to pass underneath and highlighted by a spectacular high-tech light show in the evening, it's only one part of the ongoing regeneration of Newcastle's riverside area. Open to cyclists and pedestrians (no motor traffic), it links the two alternative C2C routes along the River Tyne - Hadrian's Way along the north bank and the Keelmans' Way along the south bank, allowing C2Cers a spectacular switch between the two. A few bridge facts show the incredible nature of this achievement: It has been compared to a giant eyelid as the world-first tilting mechanism allows the bottom 'lid' to pivot up towards the upper supporting arch. Its 413feet (126 metre) length has been made to a tolerance of 1/8 of an inch (3mm) and it towers 164 feet (50 metres) above the river. It takes about 4 minutes for each opening and closing. It cost £22 million - half paid for with lottery money. It weighs 850 tonnes and contains enough steel to make 64 double decker buses.

Other bridges near city centre make for a spectacular riverscape, and from west to east are: **Redheugh Road Bridge** (1900); **King Edward Railway Bridge** (1906); **Queen Elizabeth II - Metro bridge**; **High Level Bridge** (1849) - railway, road and foot passengers. Designed by Robert Stephenson and one of the wonders of the Railway Age; **Hydraulic Swing Bridge** (1876) One of the first large opening bridges in the world. It turns on a pivot whose centre is the small blue tower; **Tyne Road Bridge** (1928), suspended by the huge suspension arch, symbol of Newcastle; last but not least is the Gateshead Millennium Bridge.

SOUTH BANK ROUTE Also known as the **Keelmans Way** route, this has been much improved from the time when it had the reputation of being poorly surfaced and difficult to navigate. It stretches from the Scotswood Bridge to the **Tyne Tunnel** where it reunites with Hadrians Way (NCN 72) on the north bank. It is signed as NCN14. After passing the Metro Centre and the incredible wooden construction of **Dunston Staithes** (coal loading jetty claimed to be the biggest wooden structure in the world) you carry on past the numerous bridges to come to the vast silvery contours of **The Sage** music venue which has a cafe and shop (0191) 443 4666 ⌨www.thesagegteshead.org Next along is the **BALTIC Centre for Contemporary Art** (0191) 4781810 ⌨www.balticmill.com Based on the former Baltic Flour Mill, the new centre houses changing displays, with the added attractions of a rooftop viewing gallery and restaurant plus a riverside cafe-bar. **Bede's World** in Jarrow is a museum based around this famous medieval monk's living place (0191) 4892106.

Crossing the Millennium Eye bridge with the Baltic Exchange arts complex in the background

87

Newcastle's centre boasts a wealth of attractions. The **Quayside** area of Newcastle is famous for its Sunday morning open market.

Trinity Maritime Centre is a restored ships' chandlers warehouses, including museum. (0191) 2614691 **The Guildhall** contains the magnificent Merchants' Court. **Bessie Surtees' House** 17th century timber-framed building. Named after a lady who eloped from here. (0191) 2691200

Castle Keep is part of the castle built between 1172 and 1178 by Henry II. The original castle gave its name to the city. **Black Gate** was added to the castle in 1247. Guarded the only level approach to the castle. Passing through the gate is the Heron Pit, an underground prison. St **Nicholas' Cathedral** has a remarkably beautiful 15th century 'crown' spire. The only other in the UK in this style is in Edinburgh. Inside are the Collingwood Monument and the brass lectern. Nearly destroyed by Scottish troops during the Civil War but the Mayor surrounded the tower with Scottish POWs to stop it being fired upon. **Central Station** is an impressive creation of the Industrial Revolution with a classical facade and massive wrought iron and glass roof. Opened by Queen Victoria in 1850. Just west of the station is the **Centre for Life** housing the **Life Science Museum** (0191) 2438210, DNA, genetics and the human body presented in a fun and educational way for youngsters. **Discovery Museum** (0191) 2326789 With over £12 million spent here in the last few years the displays on the Tyne's history should be well worth a look! **St Mary's Cathedral** 19th century, Gothic style. Designed by Pugin who helped in designing the Houses of Parliament. **Blackfriars** Remains of famous 13th century monastery. Monarchy usually resided here whilst visiting Newcastle. The remains of the **city walls** were built during the reigns of Edward I and Edward II. They were maintained until the Napoleonic Wars after which they fell into disuse so only sections remain. As you would expect **Chinatown** has many fine restaurants. **Grainger Market** 19th century buildings continue as an indoor market. **Grey's Monument** Commemorates 1832 Reform Act passed under Earl Grey's premiership. **Laing Art Gallery & Museum** Paintings, silver, glass and costumes. Art on Tyneside. The **Civic Centre** is an interesting 1960s building with notable Tyne God and Swans in Flight statues. **Great North Museum** Barras Bridge houses major displays of natural history and ancient history (0191) 222 6765.

Tourist Information

NEWCASTLE TOURIST INFORMATION 8 - 9, Central Arcade NE1 5BQ (0191) 2778000 and The Guildhall, Quayside NE1 3AF (0191) 2778000
🖥 www.newcastle.gov.uk

MARKET DAYS Grainger covered market Mon-Sat. Quayside Market Sunday mornings Farmers' Market, by Grey's Monument - first Friday every month

GATESHEAD INFORMATION CENTRE Central library Prince Consort Road NE8 4LN (0191) 4338420 🖥 www.visitnewcastlegateshead.co.uk

NORTH SHIELDS TIC Royal Quays Coble Dene (0191) 2005895
🖥 www.visitnewcastlegateshead.co.uk

WHITLEY BAY TIC Park Rd NE26 1EJ is about 2.5 miles north of Tynemouth (0191) 2008535 🖥 www.visitnewcastlegateshead.co.uk

Bike Shops

CYCLE CENTRE 250 Shields Road Byker Newcastle upon Tyne NE6 1DX
(0191) 2651472 ⌨www.cyclecentreuk.co.uk 🚲1 mile

EDINBURGH BICYCLE CO-OPERATIVE 5 - 7 Union Road Byker Newcastle
upon Tyne NE6 1EH (0191) 2658619 ⌨www.edinburghbicycle.com
🚲1 mile

HALFORDS Unit 3A Newgate Centre Newgate Street Newcastle upon Tyne
NE1 5RE (0191) 2699470 🚲0.5 miles

RIDE 259 Scotswood Road Newcastle upon Tyne NE4 7AW (0191) 2723386
⌨www.ridecycles.co.uk 🚲near route

M STEEL CYCLES 6-10 Bowsden Terr. South Gosforth NE3 1RX
Newcastle upon Tyne (0191) 2851251 ⌨www.msteelcycles.co.uk 🚲2.85 miles

PEDAL INN 172 Albert Road Jarrow NE32 5JA (0191) 4286190
⌨www.pedalinn.co.uk 🚲0.25 miles

WHIPTAIL CYCLES 3 Livingstone View Tynemouth NE30 2PL
(0191) 2572212 ⌨www.whiptailcycles.co.uk 🚲0.7 miles

See chapter 5A for Consett Bike Shops

NEWCASTLE TO TYNEMOUTH The Tyne Estuary gradually opens out as you
near journey's end. The route runs right through **Segedunum Roman Fort
Museum** (0191) 2369347 which has both excavations and reconstructions of
the eastern terminus of Hadrian's Wall as well as a viewing tower. **Royal Quays**
is an enormous shopping and housing redevelopment area. Look out for the
viewpoint in Redburn Dene park. **Wet'n'Wild** (0191) 2961333 at Royal Quays
has slides, chutes and waves as well as a swimming pool. Passing through
the quayside area of North Shields you come to **Tynemouth**. The two white
towers above and on the quay are navigational aids that ships could use to
navigate a safe passage up the Tyne (done by aligning them). **Clifford's Fort**
near the Fish Quay is the remains of a seventeenth century armed fort named
after Lord Clifford of Cabal. **Black Middens** are once notorious rocks near the
Tyne entrance. Claimed 5 ships in 3 days in November 1864. The **Collingwood
Monument** This native of Newcastle took command of the fleet at Trafalgar and
continues to look over the mouth of the Tyne today. **Tynemouth Priory and
Castle** (0191) 2571090 is surrounded by curiously eroded gravestones and
overlooks your finishing point by the pier. Originally an 11th century Norman
church and developed within a castle enclosure. Percy Chantry is the only
complete part left (heavily restored). English Heritage site. April-Oct open
daily Nov-March Thursday - Monday **Blue Reef Aquarium** (0191) 2581031
has giant 'walk-through' tanks at its centre where you can see sharks and a
great variety of sea life.

INDEX
MAIN SETTLEMENTS AND FEATURES ALONG THE C2C

ARTWORK ALONG THE C2C

How do you know you're near the Open Air Museum at Beamish? Why, because there are sculpted metal cattle grazing at the side of the path of course. The National Cycle Network is home to an enormous collection of sculptures, ranging from large earthworks to humble seats. Each route has its own distinctive character reinforced by the addition of its own distinctive sculptures and artworks.

They are particularly numerous along the traffic-free stretches of trail at either end of the route; the A to Z Newcastle and Sunderland maps have sufficient detail to show most artworks on that section. Here's just a sample:

The Old Transformers - near Annfield Plain

Rolling Coal - Stadium of Light
Sunderland

King Coal, Consett - Sunderland railpath

Too Good a Challenge not to Try Again

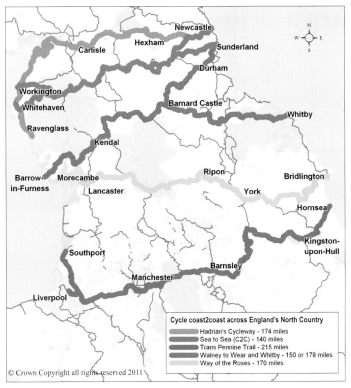

Cycle coast2coast across England's North Country

- Hadrian's Cycleway - 174 miles
- Sea to Sea (C2C) - 140 miles
- Trans Pennine Trail - 215 miles
- Walney to Wear and Whitby - 150 or 179 miles
- Way of the Roses - 170 miles

© Crown Copyright all rights reserved 2011

Hadrian's Cycleway Ravenglass – Carlisle – Hexham - Newcastle – South Shields
Trans Pennine Trail Southport - Liverpool - Barnsley - Hull - Hornsea
Walney to Wear and Whitby Barrow-in-Furness - Kendal - Barnard Castle - Durham - Sunderland and Barnard Castle - Whitby
Way of the Roses Morecambe - Lancaster - Ripon - York - Bridlington

Maps, guidebooks, t-shirts and links to route specific websites at:

www.sustrans.org.uk

sustrans

JOIN THE MOVEMENT

THE BIKE FOR ALL REASONS

Photo by Chris Hill

The **HELIOS** tandem really is the bike for all *reasons*.

Not only is it excellent to ride both as a load carrier and a tandem, but it also offers the convenience of being ultra compact. By removing the front wheel , dropping both seat posts down and quick releasing the handlebar, it fits into 180 x 60 x 22cm space. Allowing it to be fitted to a standard bike rack, or, with the seats down, into the back of most hatchback cars. The dedicated rear rack, which replaces the stoker seat post can take 4 panniers, 2 child seats, a combination of both or anything else you want to strap to it.

Circe Cycles

t | 01954 782020   e | info@circecycles.com   w | www.circecycles.com

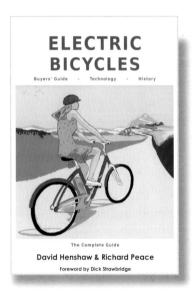

MO

EDE

& NORT CUMBRIA

EXCELLENT BOOKS

EXCELLENT BOOKS
94 BRADFORD ROAD
WAKEFIELD
WEST YORKSHIRE WF1 2AE
TEL / FAX: (01924) 315147

First Published 2000

ISBN 1-901464-07-5

Front cover photos: The track to Cross Fell (top). Above the Eden near
Pendragon Castle (bottom)
Rear cover photo: On Lady Anne's Highway above Mallerstang
Frontispiece: Near Skiddaw youth hostel

Printed in Great Britain by:
FM Repro Ltd.
Repro House, 69 Lumb Lane
Roberttown
Liversedge
West Yorkshire WF15 7NB

CONTENTS

Descending to Crossgreens (ride 15)

INTRODUCTION

WHY THE EDEN VALLEY AND NORTH CUMBRIA?

When it comes to mountain biking Cumbria is known above all else for the towering peaks of Lakeland. However, spectacular as the Lakes are, there is also a wealth of exciting and very varied riding to be found outside of the National Park. Some routes within these pages may be familiar, such as around Skiddaw and above Ullswater, but it's less likely you will have explored the delights of Mallerstang, the Cross Fell massif or the Bewcastle Fells. If not, you're missing out on a bewildering variety of splendid off-road experiences. New horizons and new experiences are out there waiting for you!

THE LANDSCAPE

The River Eden begins its life on the very edge of the Yorkshire Dales National Park, at the head of the unusually named dale of Mallerstang. It gradually mellows after passing through the spectacular scars and edges of upper Mallerstang, ever-widening as it heads north-west, sandwiched between the Pennines north of the Stainmore Gap and the peaks of Lakeland. Towards the end of its 67 mile length it turns west through Carlisle and out into the silvery and sandy expanse of the of the Solway Firth, with Scotland's Southern Uplands rising in the background to the north.

All along its course the landscape on either side of the Eden holds many treasures. Secret corners such as the Howgills and the limestone pavement country between Orton and Great Asby are a delightful contrast to the brooding presence of the Northern Pennines; the long smooth summit of Cross Fell and the accompanying 'golf ball' radar station on Great Dun Fell soon become familiar companions on rides in the area. The Lake District National Park has been well-known for decades but it was only in 1988 that 772 square miles of the North Pennines were designated an Area of Outstanding Natural Beauty making it the largest such designated area in the country.

Travelling north from the luscious lower reaches of the Eden the landscape becomes less populated and takes on a bleak beauty as it rises towards the Bewcastle Fells on the border with Scotland. More than any other part of Cumbria this is a wilderness landscape, and uniquely beautiful with it. High rainfall and poor drainage have given rise to boggy pasture dissected by unpolluted streams and rivers. The disappearance of the traditional cover of birch and alder has left swathes of wild grasses carpeting the wide open spaces.

WEATHER AND TRACK CONDITIONS

Cumbria gets more than its fair share of rain; much of the area receives over 40 inches of rain per year and the figure peaks above the Lakes at over 100 inches per year. This makes fine, sunny days especially valuable so make the most of them.

Tracks will, of course, vary massively in condition according to the weather. The majority of these rides were done in good weather in late summer, so track descriptions here reflect that period. Avoiding periods of heavy rain will not only make conditions easier for the rider but will help conserve the track surfaces. Winter mountain biking enthusiasts will already know cold, clear days when the ground is frozen hard provide excellent biking conditions. Should you venture out in such conditions you should be aware of the possibility of sheets of ice on puddles and across frozen streams which can be potentially lethal. So, in fact, the best conditions are found in the extreme opposites of our climate, either at the height of a dry summer or on cold, crisp, clear days in winter.

ACCESS

The Settle-Carlisle line provides excellent access to many of the rides. Its numerous stops pass through spectacular Dales scenery before going down the Eden Valley. The west coast line has far fewer stations, linking the major population centres of Preston, Lancaster, Penrith and Carlisle. For those coming from the Cumbrian coast the line linking Carnforth and Carlisle is useful. The map overleaf shows all stations on and around the rides. A summary of carrying bikes on trains from and to the areas follows. Bear in mind these are the official rules and in practice staff usually try and accommodate you and most people have few problems. If your schedule is tight booking ahead is reassuring though.

• **Northern Spirit** runs the line Settle-Carlisle line and services from Newcastle to Carlisle across the Tyne Gap. On the former service up to 2 bikes are allowed per train, free, and must be booked in advance. Most services from Newcastle are non-reservable and carry two bikes but you may not be allowed on at peak times. Certain services carry six bikes and are reservable. Ring (0870) 6023322 for details. A good map of all their services is on the website www.northern-spirit.co.uk

• **Virgin** operate the west coast line which passes through Preston, Lancaster, Penrith, Carlisle and Glasgow. Advance reservations are essential and cost £3.00 per bike per journey. They operate the only service between Carlisle and Penrith and although this is only a local journey reservations are still essential! Contact (0345) 222333. A full national network map is at www.virgintrains.co.uk

• **First North Western** operate the Cumbrian coastal line which includes Dalston. Space for two bikes per train on a free, non-reservable, 'first come first served basis'.

RAIL ENQUIRIES - 0345 484950

The above number is excellent for getting straightforward fare and timetable information. However, beware when asking for particular information on taking bikes on trains. Very general advice is often given and is not necessarily accurate! They may simply give you the number for the operating company concerned; in any case this is the best advice; you are better getting particular details from the operators, who will be more precise.

• **The Sherpa Van Project** is a back up service for those on the cyclists' C2C and the walkers' Coast to Coast routes, amongst others. It visits many of the towns in this guide. General info: Tel (0181) 5694101. Website www.sherpavan.com

USING THIS GUIDE AND OTHER MAPS

Although you should be able to complete all the routes in this book using the directions and route maps within these pages, an OS map of at least 1:50,000 scale and a compass are vital safety aids should you become disorientated or lost. If you stray off the route these tools will help you get back on course. Excellent as these maps are, you still need to be competent in using them to interpret the landscape; practice makes perfect and there are also many good books around on mountain safety which include details on map reading.

Ride introductions detail the relevant maps for that ride but the 1:50,000 list below gives a summary of all the maps needed to complete all rides. The 1:25,000 list details OS Outdoor Leisure maps which only cover some rides. 1:25,000 Pathfinder maps are not detailed as these are being discontinued.

1:50,000 OS Landranger Maps

98 Wensleydale & Upper Wharfedale   91 Appleby-in-Westmorland
90 Penrith & Keswick   85 Carlisle & Solway Firth
86 Haltwhistle, Brampton & Bewcastle

1:25,000 Outdoor Leisure

19 Howgill Fells & Upper Eden Valley   5 English Lakes North Eastern Area
4 English Lakes North Western Area   31 North Pennines
43 Hadrian's Wall

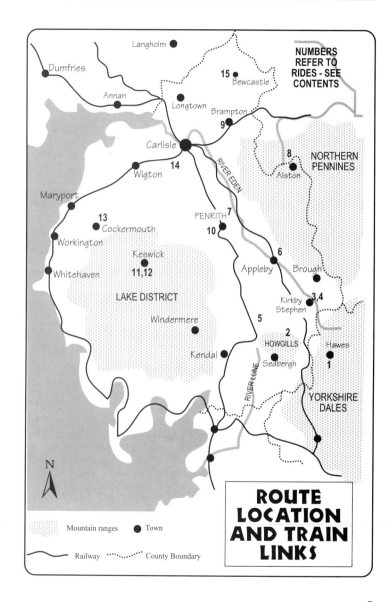

NUMBERS REFER TO RIDES - SEE CONTENTS

Langholm

Dumfries

Annan

Longtown

Brampton

9

15 Bewcastle

Carlisle

RIVER EDEN

8 NORTHERN PENNINES

Alston

Wigton

14

Maryport

13 Cockermouth

PENRITH 7

10

Workington

Keswick

6

Whitehaven

11,12

Appleby

Brough

LAKE DISTRICT

Kirkby Stephen

3,4

Windermere

5

2

HOWGILLS

Hawes

Kendal

Seabergh

1

RIVER LUNE

YORKSHIRE DALES

N

Mountain ranges ● Town

Railway ········· County Boundary

ROUTE LOCATION AND TRAIN LINKS

EQUIPMENT

Clearly the most important piece of equipment is a bike that you can ride comfortably and safely. All the routes in this guide are really only suitable for mountain bikes. You should know how to do basic maintenance and carry the following basic tools suitable for the jobs described. Because of the rougher conditions of mountain biking compared to road biking more maintenance is bound to be required:

* *Puncture repair kit ,spare inner tubes and air pump*; for burst inner tubes
* *Tyre levers;* for burst inner tubes
* *Range of spanners*; changing of wheel if not quick release. Other common adjustments e.g. if pedal becomes loose
* *Small screwdriver*; adjusting gear mechanisms.
* *Adjustable spanner*; will fit a number of bike nuts if they work loose.
* *Allen keys* ; to fit various adjustments, handlebar stem, seat post, v-brakes etc.
* *Chainsplitter*; this tool not only takes chains apart but you <u>may</u> be able to rejoin your chain if it breaks whilst riding.
* *Pliers*; for tightening brake and gear cables.
* *Small change and friend's phone number*; for when you are utterly stuck because of mechanical failure of bike/car !
* Although not strictly a tool a *bivi bag / survival bag* for remote or higher altitude routes is highly recommended.
N.B. There are special bike 'combination tools' that contain a number of the above tools and save a lot of weight e.g. Cooltool or Ritchey combination tool.

Other useful clothes items are;

* Padded shorts or three quarter length bottoms depending on the weather. Special cycling shorts help to prevent saddle soreness.
* Durable footwear with a chunky sole to grip the pedal. Some pedal systems have clips or the facility to 'screw' the underneath of a sole to the pedal which can be useful to keep your feet on the pedals over rough ground. Practice disengaging your feet quickly from the system so you can use it safely.
* Good waterproof, breathable tops and bottoms.
* Waterproof cycling gloves. (Fingerless ones are very useful in warmer weather).

You heat up quickly on a bike so you should have the capability to take off and add a couple of layers of clothing and keep dry spares in panniers or a small backpack. Too much weight or too large a backpack will destabilise you.

MAINTENANCE

If you set off with a well-maintained bike the chances are that you won't need any of the tools or spares you take. A bike in good condition is especially important for such a long distance route. The most basic check should include the following list and if in any doubt about the state of your bike get it checked over properly at a good bike shop.

Important safety checks - do not neglect them!

Brake check - you should only be able to squeeze in front and rear brake levers a centimetre or two and braking response should be nice and sharp. Check brake blocks aren't rubbing on wheel rims, or even worse, tyres.
Brake cables - check that front and rear brake cables are not fraying. If they are replace them immediately.
Brake blocks - check that when you brake the blocks hit only the wheel rim, not the tyre, and that there is plenty of wear left in the block.
Tyres - should be inflated to manufacturer's recommended pressure (as a rough guide you should just be able to depress the tyre when squeezing it). Check there is adequate tread.
 Make sure the following are **lubricated**: front and rear brake pivots, moving parts of front and rear gear mechanisms, chain, brake lever pivots, entry and exit points of all cables. Keep these points well-lubricated during the ride.
 Appropriate **screws and bolts** should be tight and you should check all gears are shifting properly.

For a full guide to buying and maintaining a bike see Haynes 'The Bike Book'.

NAVIGATION

Map and compass are vital pieces of safety equipment. If you follow the directions in the book accurately (and presuming the features used as direction finders are not altered) you shouldn't have any problems. However, should you become lost these two aids are the key to finding your way back home quickly and safely. There are plenty of guides on safety in the mountains which give you accurate instructions on map reading and other important techniques. Bike computers can help in determining distances and average speed along with a wealth of other statistics of your journey. The higher up you go, the further you are from a main settlement or phonebox and the harsher the weather conditions, the more potentially vital will become your map reading technique. Its importance cannot be stressed enough.

Near Bullcleugh Gate (ride 15)

THE MOUNTAIN BIKE CODE OF CONDUCT

(With the author's own additions in italics)

RIGHTS OF WAY

* Bridleways - open to cyclists but you must give way to walkers and horse riders. (*Legally they should be signposted at junctions with public roads but this isn't always the case. Also note horses, especially young nervous ones can be very scared of bikes. When they are coming in the opposite direction it's best to stop. When you approach from behind give a gentle 'excuse me' if you think the riders haven't heard you. If you scare a horse it can bolt causing injury to the rider or those nearby)*
* Byways - Usually unsurfaced tracks open to cyclists. As well as walkers and cyclists you may meet occasional vehicles which also have a right of access. *This classification also now includes RUPPS (roads used as public paths) which no longer exist as a separate category.*
* Public footpaths - no right to cycle exists.

Look out for posts or waymarking arrows pointing off the highway (blue for bridleways, red for byways and yellow for footpaths).

NB The above rights do not apply in Scotland.

OTHER ACCESS

* Open land - on most upland, moorland and farmland cyclists normally have no right of access without the express permission of the landowner.
* Towpaths - a British Waterways cycling permit is required for cyclists wishing to use their canal towpaths. Many sections are for walkers only.
* Pavements - cycling is not permitted on pavements
* Designated cycle paths - look out for designated cycle paths or bicycle routes which may be found in urban areas, on forestry commission land, disused railway lines or other open spaces.
* Cyclists must adhere to the Highway Code.

Keep to tracks where you know you have a legal right to cycle; mountain biking has gained a bad name with other countryside users because of a few irresponsible riders. There have even been calls for legislation to ban it!

FOLLOW THE COUNTRY CODE.

* Enjoy the countryside and respect its life and work.
* Guard against all risk of fire.
* **Fasten all gates (famers in the area have made a special plea!)**
* Keep dogs under close control.
* Keep to rights of way across farmland.
* Use gates and stiles to cross fences, hedges and walls.
* Leave livestock, crops and machinery alone.
* Take your litter home.
* Help to keep all water clean.
* Protect wildlife, plants and trees.
* Take special care on country roads.
* Make no unnecessary noise.

SAFETY

* Ensure that your bike is safe to ride and prepared for all emergencies.
* You are required by law to display working lights after dark (front and rear).
* Always carry some form of identification.
* Always tell someone where you are going.
* Learn to apply the basic principles of first aid.
* Reflective materials on your clothes or bike can save your life. *(Obviously this applies doubly to road sections)*
* For safety on mountains refer to specialist publications.
* Ride under control when going downhill since this is often when serious accidents occur.
* If you intend to ride fast off road it is advisable to wear a helmet.
* Particular care should be taken on unstable or wet surfaces.

Careful pre-ride checks = a relaxing ride!

RIGHTS OF WAY

Although the legal position is set out in the code of conduct above the situation on the ground may not be that simple.

There are many minor roads shown on maps but their status is not clear from the map alone and may need further research. Bridleways may be shown on a map but may not be evident when you look for them or may be obstructed when you try to ride along them. Similarly many rights of way that exist for bikes may not be shown on the map.

These problems are solved by this guide; all routes were fully legal at the time of going to press and their legality has been researched extensively by the author. However it is still strongly recommended to take the appropriate map and a compass in case you happen to become lost. Up to date OS Outdoor Leisure maps are the most detailed showing features such as individual fields. The book directions and maps will complement these maps, although bear in mind occasionally bridleways that may not be marked as such on these maps are used.

Please stick to the tracks indicated. In particular mountain bikers going down footpaths and private roads in some areas have caused a severe backlash against the sport and have prompted calls to Parliament to have it banned !

KEY TO ROUTE MAPS

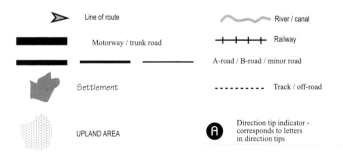

Line of route		River / canal
Motorway / trunk road		Railway
		A-road / B-road / minor road
Settlement		Track / off-road
UPLAND AREA		Direction tip indicator - corresponds to letters in direction tips

USEFUL ADDRESSES

Cyclists Touring Club, Cotterell House, 69 Meadrow, Godalming, Surrey GU7 3HS 01483 417217. This once traditional organisation has now grown to incorporate off-road cycling, including 'hardcore' mountain biking, and has a Mountain Bike Development Officer. They also have a list of regional off-road access coordinators.
British Cycling Federation, National Cycling Centre, Stuart Street, Manchester M11 4DQ 0161 2302301. E-mail: 101701.2660@Compuserve.Com. **British Mountain Biking** is the off-road branch of this organisation.
Rough Stuff Fellowship 18 Water St, Bollington, Macclesfield, Chesire SK10 5HF 01625 573873. For those who enjoy exploring off-road tracks.
Youth Hostels Association Trevelyan House, 8 St. Stephens Hill, St Albans, Herts AL1 2DY 01727 855215
Byways & Bridleways Trust PO Box 117, Newcastle Upon Tyne NE3 5YT 0191 2364086

TOURIST INFORMATION OFFICES

Hawes, Dales Countryside Museum, Station Yard DL8 3NT 01969 667450
Kirkby Stephen, Market Street CA17 4QN 017683 71199
Appleby, Moothall, Boroughgate CA16 6XD 017683 51177
Keswick, Moot Hall, Market Square CA12 5JR 017687 72645
Penrith, Robinsons School, Middlegate CA11 7PT 01768 867466
Pooley Bridge, The Square CA10 2NW 017684 86530 (seasonal opening)
Cockermouth, Town Hall, Market Street CA13 9NP 01900 822634
Carlisle, Old Town Hall, Green Market CA3 8JH 01228 625600
Alston, The Railway Station CA9 3JB 01434 381696
Brampton, Moot Hall, Market Place CA8 1RW 016977 3433 (seasonal opening)

MOUNTAIN RESCUE

Dial 999 and tell the operator the required service. Give the number of the phone and stay there until the emergency services ring you back. Make sure you give your location as accurately as possible.

The old stone surface shows through on parts of Lady Anne's Highway (ride 1)

1 HAWES - KIRKBY STEPHEN

Start Hawes town centre   **Grid ref** 874898

Distance 30km / 19 miles in one direction. Double this for a return journey to Hawes

Time Allowed 4-5 hours one way   **Off road riding**   65%

Gradient Difficulty *Easy - Moderate - **Difficult** - Very Difficult*

Track Surface / Roads Lady Anne's Highway varies between superb, well-drained sections over flat limestone pavement to more boggy, rutted sections which may prove a struggle to ride. After a long, difficult push up to Cotter End there is some superb riding on a firm, short grass carpet with simply staggering views over the Upper Ure towards Garsdale Head. On the descent into Mallerstang watch out for ruts and large stones; definitely one for 'technical riders' with at least front suspension! There should be some track improvements in terms of drainage and surface to Lady Anne's Highway during 2000.

OS Maps
1:50,000 Landranger 98 Wensleydale & 91 Appleby in Westmorland
1:25,000 Outdoor Leisure
2 Yorkshire Dales South & Western & 19 Howgill Fells

Access Garsdale station, on the Settle - Carlisle line, is some 6 miles from Hawes centre along the A684. In fact, this main road passes the route where Lady Anne's Highway joins the road, so if you want to miss out the road section from Hawes you can join it here, at the start of the climb to Cotter End.

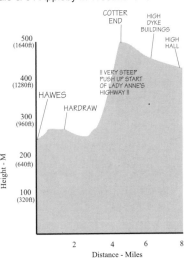

ALONG THE WAY

• **Hawes** Wensleydale's market town, and a tourist 'honeypot' in season. The cascading Duerley Beck, passing through the eastern end of the town, gives it much of its character. Also at this end of town, in the graveyard of St Margarets Church, is the Hawes Junction Memorial, commemorating a 1910 fatal accident on the Settle-Carlisle line. The graveyard also contains many unmarked graves of navvies who worked on the line. Visitor attractions include the Dales Countryside Museum alongside the National Park centre, ropemakers and the Wensleydale creamery. Banks, pubs and food stores are found along the main street alongside more specialised local shops.

• **Hardraw Force** Impressive waterfall, found behind the Green Dragon Inn at Hardraw. Small admission charge. Occasional band concerts are held in this spectacular setting. Tearoom in Hardraw.

• **Lady Anne's Highway** From Cotter End the route follows the line of this probable prehistoric highway. Its name comes from later use by Lady Anne Clifford who would travel along it in her horse litter along with her servants. It gives superb views over the upper Ure towards Dandymire Viaduct. After crossing over the River Eden, near its source at Hell Gill Bridge, the Highway drops down into Mallerstang, with fine views of Wild Boar Fell on the left.

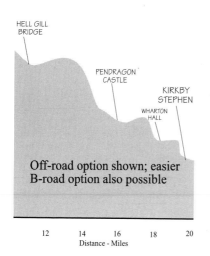

HELL GILL
BRIDGE

PENDRAGON
CASTLE

KIRKBY
STEPHEN

WHARTON
HALL

Off-road option shown; easier
B-road option also possible

12   14   16   18   20
Distance - Miles

DIRECTIONS

A - B From the centre of Hawes head east down Market St. The road bends L to become one-way. Just before the turning for the information centre go L, signed for Muker and Hardraw. Cross over the River Ure and climb to a T-junction where you go L. Stay on this road to meet the A684 and go R for Sedbergh and Kirkby Stephen. Take the first R, signed 'Cotterdale Only' and immediately on turning cross a cattle grid and head L, off the road, onto the byway that is known as Lady Anne's Highway.

You can trace the rough line of a grassy track as it heads in a straight line to join a wall on your L. From here it ascends steeply and diagonally to the R, aiming just to the L of the plantation at Cotter End. Superb views over the head of Wensleydale open up behind you. Through a bridleway gate pick up a snaking track to pass an old limekiln before the track flattens and becomes a grassy carpet, following the line of a wall on your L. There are stunning views over the upper Ure towards Dandymire Viaduct. Accompany this wall for about 4km as it passes 3 sets of abandoned buildings, after which the wall drops away. You stay on the well-defined track to come to Hell Gill Bridge over a ravine housing the Eden.

B - C After this bridge follow a lovely wide grass track to a superb viewpoint over Mallerstang by a new concrete sculpture. From here the track descends on a rutted, rocky surface to the B6259 in the bottom of Mallerstang (improvements planned for 2000). Head R onto the road. Pendragon Castle comes into view on your L. From here you have the option of carrying straight on, on the B road, into Kirkby Stephen or turning L by the castle to follow the off-road option into Kirkby Stephen.

If you want to follow the off-road option full directions from the castle are given in ride 3. If continuing on the road you will enter Kirkby Stephen by going through Nateby, staying on the B road through this settlement. You will meet the main street in Kirkby Stephen just after passing the Temperance Hall on the R. Turn R onto the main road to get to the heart of the town, centred around the old Market Place.

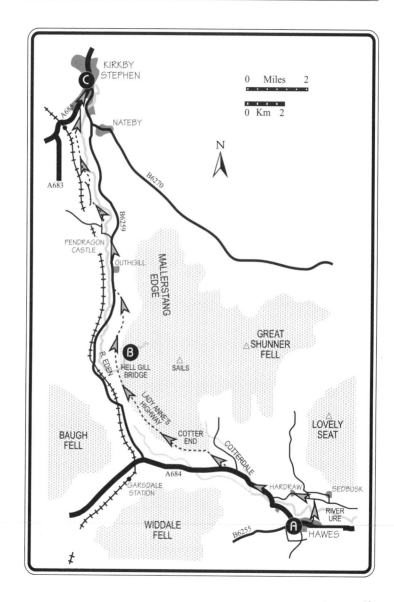

2 WEST OF MALLERSTANG

Start Ravenstonedale, outside the village school   **Grid ref** 722042

Distance 32km / 20 miles

Time Allowed 4-5 hours   **Off road riding** 45%

Gradient Difficulty *Easy - Moderate - **Difficult** - Very Difficult*

Track Surface / Roads A clear green lane leads from Adamthwaite Farm and through Narthwaite before field sections and a narrow path through Murthwaite Park Woods. The section before Narthwaite starts off well as a grassy, shelf-like track with occassional boggy sections. Eventually it disappears into a grassy ditch where you must pick your way round the side then drops down a rocky descent to Narthwaite. From Stennerskeugh an excellent track leads over the northern shoulder of Wild Boar Fell before a precipitous and stunning descent into Mallerstang.

OS Maps
1:50,000 Landranger 98 Wensleydale & 91 Appleby in Westmorland
1:25,000 Outddor Leisure 2´ Yorkshire Dales South & Western & 19 Howgill Fells

Access The nearest rail access to Ravenstonedale is at Kirkby Stephen station on the Settle Carlisle line, some 5km from the start on the A685 (beware of fast traffic).

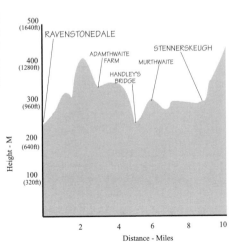

ALONG THE WAY

• **Ravenstonedale** is a beautiful village with an old world feel. For refreshments choose from the Black Swan Hotel and the Kings Head Hotel.
• **Stennerskeugh and Fell End Clouds** are outstanding limestone outcrops before the ascent towards **Wild Boar Fell**. The spectacular 'tabletop'of this fell dominates the skyline on the long climb to the highest point on the route. On coming over its northern shoulder a spectacular view opens up across Mallerstang towards Hangingstone Scar and Mallerstang Edge.

Mallerstang (ride 2)

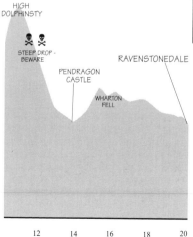

HIGH DOLPHINSTY

STEEP DROP - BEWARE

RAVENSTONEDALE

PENDRAGON CASTLE

WHARTON FELL

12   14   16   18   20
Distance - Miles

DIRECTIONS

A - B Start in Ravenstonedale at the small parking area in front of the village school. Head south east and bend 90 degrees R past the Black Swan Hotel. Head up the main street to where the road bends L on leaving the village. Go R here, signed for Artlegarth and Adamthwaite and marked as a dead end. Follow this road for about 4.5km, ignoring the L split for Artlegarth. Enter the farm buildings at Adamthwaite and go through two gates to head down a walled green lane (possibly very boggy at the bottom). This develops into an excellent green, shelf-like track on the hillside before the lane drops into an impassable ditch, where you must pick your way around the side. A rocky descent then leads into the cluster of buildings at Narthwaite.

Stay on the main track through Narthwaite and bend L to keep descending. The track bends R down to Handley's Bridge and you may be tempted to descend all the way on this good surface. However, the line of the bridleway continues straight on at this bend and into the field ahead. Head across the middle of the field and over the ford in the bottom corner to enter Murthwaite Park Woods. DISMOUNT HERE AND PROCEED SLOWLY - THIS IS A SITE OF SPECIAL SCIENTIFIC INTEREST SO BE DOUBLY SURE TO RESPECT THE ENVIRONMENT. In the woods a path heads L and steeply uphill to emerge into what becomes open reedy pasture. Follow a straight line to join a wall on your R which leads to Murthwaite farm buildings.

B - C Through Murthwaite farm buildings pick up the drive which heads downhill to meet the A683 by a small chapel. Head straight across the road onto the byway marked for High Dovengill and climb to meet a minor road. L here to follow this gloriously quiet road under the limestone outcrops of Fell End and Stennerskeugh Clouds. On meeting the A-road again head R and take the next R turn signed Stennerskeugh. Bend L in front of the grand gates and about 80m past a castle-like folly standing behind a wall go R onto the bridleway marked for Mallerstang. Ascend and go through the gate and pick up an excellent well-compacted track in front of you. The line of the track is extremely clear for the next 2.5km or so as it climbs steadily, crossing three small streams on the way. Eventually you meet a gate that leads onto the plateau between Wild Boar Fell and Little Fell.

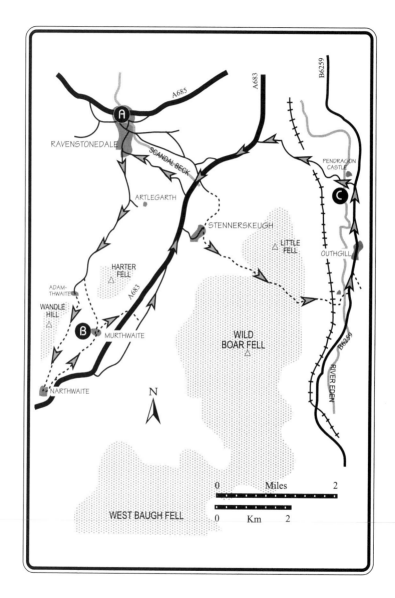

23

The crags at the northern end of Wild Boar Fell are up to your R but don't be tempted to head across the gently rising ground that heads towards them. Almost immediately through the gate a less well defined track drops quickly down, hugging the side of quite a steep drop (EXTRA CARE REQUIRED IF RIDING THIS SECTION). The line of the track is briefly lost to cross the hummocky edge of a limestone pavement but the good quality track is easliy visible ahead of you.

This track drops down, with intermittent steep sections, to cross a beck before hairpinning under the Settle-Carlisle railway line. The clear track passes Hazelgill Farm to join the farm drive to meet the B6259 in the bottom of Mallerstang. Go L and head north up the valley to Pendragon Castle.

C - A Take the L turn at Pendragon Castle to climb over Wharton Fell before dropping and climbing to meet the A683 again. Go L onto this main road, passing a picturesque tarn on the L. Take the first minor road on the R (easy to miss). Ignore the road that joins from the L but take the next R turn onto an extremely minor road. At a T-junction go L to come to a more major T-junction. R here brings you back into Ravenstonedale over the River Rawthey. Go R by the Black Swan Hotel and back to the start point.

Near Adamthwaite Farm in the Howgills (ride 2)

Birkett Common (ride 3)

3 PENDRAGON CASTLE

Start Kirkby Stephen centre   **Grid ref** 775087

Distance 17km / 10.5 miles   **Time Allowed** 2-3 hours

Off road riding 50%

Gradient Difficulty _Easy_ - Moderate - Difficult - Very Difficult

Track Surface / Roads A wide variety of green lanes, mainly in good condition, although some can become overgrown in summer so take full length bottoms! A superb moorland track leads around Birkett Common. There are a couple of easy to follow field sections, one leaving the road at Hartley then another before joining the good quality concreted entrance track to Wharton Hall. There are very brief road sections along the busy A685 that runs through Kirkby Stephen. You follow the B6259 for several kilometres between Nateby and Pendragon Castle. This beautiful road should normally be fairly quiet as it's not a major carrier of trans-Pennine traffic. However, you should watch out for fast motorbikes on summer weekends as they seem to favour its crests and dips!

OS Maps
1:50,000 Landranger 91 Appleby in Westmorland
1:25,000 Outdoor Leisure 19 Howgill Fells & Upper Eden Valley

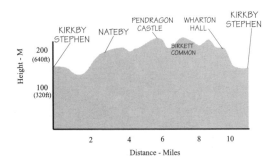

Access There is a station at Kirkby Stephen although this is about 2.5 km from the town centre. It is on the beautiful Settle-Carlisle line which you can see from many points on the route.

ALONG THE WAY

• A huge variety of architecture crowds the streets of **Kirkby Stephen**. The centre is the **market square** and the ring of cobblestones here marks out the area where the traditional 'sport' of bull baiting once took place. The fine old church of **St Stephen** houses many old stone monuments including the Norse Cross of Loki, showing a bound devil. The churchyard is entered through a set of attractive cloisters. **Stenkrith Park**, south of the town, has dramatic cascades on the River Eden. There are plenty of cafes and pubs in the town centre. Bike Hire at **Kirkby Pet and Fishing Supplies**, just off the market Square, (01768) 372314. Cycle spares and repairs at **Stephen McWhirters** in the Station Yard (01768) 371052 / 372442.

• There is a tea room in Hartley.

• **The Black Bull** in Nateby serves food.

• **Pendragon Castle** lies in the lonely **Mallerstang Dale**. Tradition has it that this castle was built by King Arthur's father but it is in fact Norman. It was razed by the Scots in 1541 and rebuilt in the 17th century by one of the most powerful northern families, the Cliffords. It has since fallen into its present ruined state.

• The route passes right next to **Wharton Hall**, sitting in isolated splendour next to the River Eden. It is now a farmhouse and an Ancient Monument but was once the residence of the local aristocrats. It dates from the 14th century and was added to and refurbished over the next 400 or so years.

• At several places on the route you cross the now defunct **Tebay to Darlington Railway**, which once ran across the Pennines to link two counties and passed through Kirkby Stephen. A branch line also led north up the Eden Valley. If access were legalised and the surface improved it would make an excellent all purpose off-road link, Sustrans style. Its current state is certainly a pity.

Pendragon Castle (ride 3)

DIRECTIONS

A - B Head north from the tourist information office in Kirkby Stephen and about 80m past the church go R down Hartley Road and over a small bridge. Follow the road to a T-junction in Hartley and go R. Go through Hartley to the small bridge by the telephone box where you go R. In about 40m go R onto the tarmac path by Saltpie Hall. Through the gate follow the L-hand side of the field then descend between hillock and barn to the small bridge in the far corner. Across the bridge follow the woodland path to emerge by the entrances to two fields. Pick up the narrow green lane between the two fields (easy to miss if overgrown in summer). Follow to descend over a ford and climb a rocky, sunken lane before the track widens and levels to cross the line of a disused railway. A gentle descent leads to a split by a ford. Bear L to emerge at a road in Nateby. Go R and uphill to a T-junction with the B6259 in Nateby.

B - C Go L onto the B6259 and stay on it out of Nateby, passing the Black Bull pub on the R. This becomes a superb, undulating B-road leading up Mallerstang Dale. The daunting ridge of Mallerstang Edge draws closer, paralleling the road up to the L. About 5km after joining this B-road take the first R turn in front of Pendragon Castle ruins. Cross the River Eden then bend and climb past houses at Cocklake to take the R onto the track just over the cattle grid signed for Wharton. This is a superb off-road section with great views back down the valley. In just over a kilometre come to a split by the river and go L to follow the line of telegraph poles. In a further kilometre or so the track goes through a gate and turns 90 degrees L to Croop House (remains of Lammerside Castle in the field to the R). At Croop House go R onto the road. Climb for just under a kilometre to come to Bull Ghyll house with its 'own' public postbox and telephone!

C - A Head R at Bull Ghyll down the green lane enclosed by walls. This is difficult but rideable (possibly overgrown in summer). At the end of the green lane carry on to descend down the R-hand side of the next three fields (two small then one large) to join the track above the very impressive Wharton Hall. Head R on this track to descend and bend L between the hall and farm buildings joining a concrete section road. This joins a public road at Halfpenny House then descends to the A685 (fast and busy). Head R on the main road, back into Kirkby Stephen centre.

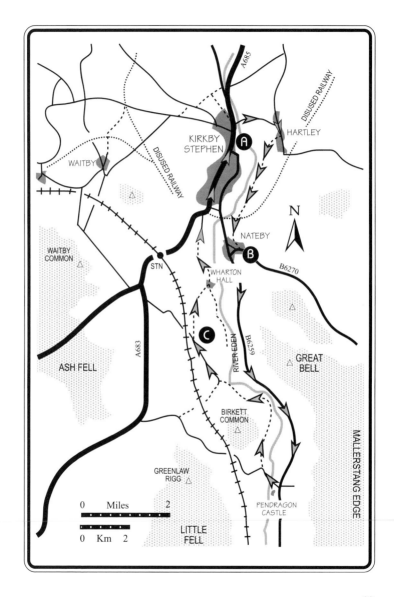

KIRKBY STEPHEN

A

HARTLEY

DISUSED RAILWAY

DISUSED RAILWAY

A685

WAITBY

WAITBY COMMON

STN

NATEBY

B

B6270

N

WHARTON HALL

C

RIVER EDEN

B6259

GREAT BELL

ASH FELL

A683

BIRKETT COMMON

MALLERSTANG EDGE

GREENLAW RIGG

0   Miles   2

0   Km   2

LITTLE FELL

PENDRAGON CASTLE

4 SMARDALE AND CROSBY GARRETT FELLS

Start Kirkby Stephen centre

Grid ref 775087

Distance 28km / 17.5 miles

Time Allowed 4-5 hours

Off road riding 57%

Gradient Difficulty *Easy - Moderate - **Difficult** - Very Difficult*

Track Surface / Roads The walled green lanes leading out of Kirkby Stephen can be somewhat overgrown with nettles in summer but underneath the surface is very flat and fast, so if bare skin is covered up you can actually ride these! In any case, the more these good quality lanes are used the less will be the problem with undergrowth in high summer. A rocky track ascends Smardale Fell and a small field section precedes an increasingly good green track down to Smardale Bridge. Several roughly defined bridleway tracks lead onto Crosby Garrett Fell where you pick up an excellently-surfaced track to descend into Crosby Garrett. The Soulby-Winton by-road is largely well-surfaced track.

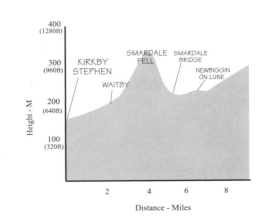

OS Maps
1:50,000 Landranger 91 Appleby in Westmorland
1:25,000 Outdoor Leisure 19 Howgill Fells & Upper Eden Valley

Access There is a station at Kirkby Stephen although this is about 2.5 km from the town centre. It is on the beautiful Settle-Carlisle line which you can see from many points on the route.

ALONG THE WAY

• For details about **Kirkby Stephen** and the **Tebay - Darlington railway** see route 3.
• Smardale Bridge crosses the fascinating **Scandal Beck**. Descending to the bridge various features of the beck come into view; a limestone scar known as 'Witches Stride', quarry workings, a massive kiln and finally the viaduct that carried the disused Tebay - Darlington railway comes into view. If you secure your bike at the bridge you can follow a permissive footpath onto the viaduct for superb views.
• Both **Smardale** and **Crosby Garrett Fells** give superb vistas of the **Northern Pennines** and **The Howgills**.
• **Crosby Garrett** is a sleepy village grouped around a beck and appears untouched by tourism and tweeness alike. Many of the dated lintels show buildings stretching back to the 17th century.

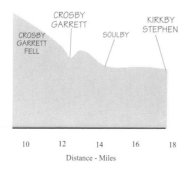

31

• The **Settle-Carlisle Railway** is seen close up as you pass under the viaduct at Crosby Garrett. The line opened in 1876 after seven years work and it was designed to link the area with the industrial Midlands. It is incredible to think that the line was threatened with closure in the 1980s. Its continued use is surely the best monument to the labourers who worked on it (indeed, it claimed the lives of many of them). The threatened closure and consequent outcry may have been a good thing as they played a part in the line's subsequent increase in popularity.

The beautiful Scandal Beck (ride 4)

DIRECTIONS

A - B From outside the tourist information office in Kirkby Stephen head north along the A685. Immediately after the garage and CO-OP supermarket on the left, turn L down the concrete bridleway track for Green Syke Lane. Come alongside the cemetery immediately on your R. The track carries straight on and narrows, hemmed in by walls. At the next track T-junction go L, continuing on a narrow green lane, which shortly widens to a good track then meets the road at a T-junction. Go R and in about 40m L, onto the bridleway marked for Sandwath Bridge. Follow to the next road T-junction and go R over Sandwath Bridge. In about 50m go R and pass Moorlands Farm on the R. Go L by Waitby House onto an unsigned byway and follow the good track to a fork. Go L to cross the line of the old Tebay-Darlington railway. The track becomes metalled and enters the tiny village of Waitby. Head straight on past the first grass triangle and at the second go R for Smardale.

Ignore the L turn past the small disused school and carry straight on to descend towards the impressive turrets of Smardale Hall and go L down the side of the hall, signed as a bridleway to Smardale Fell. Pass under the Settle-Carlisle railway and at the road's end pass through the gate to follow bridleway signs for Brownber and the A685. Immediately through the gate follow the steep track up the R-hand side of the field. This levels out and heads away from the trees and wall to pass through a gate. In the next field stay by the wall on the R as you lose the track but in the next field the rough line of a track starts again. Follow this track, roughly parallel to the long wall on the R. The Howgills appear ahead of you and you descend to a rights of way junction. Stay on the track by the wall and simply follow this for a further 2km or so, when it bends R through a gate & descends rockily to the beautiful Smardale Bridge. Over the bridge carry on in a straight line to pass through a gate and climb on a track along the L-hand side of a large field. Over the rise the track improves and descends to bend L at Friars Bottom Farm, where it becomes metalled.

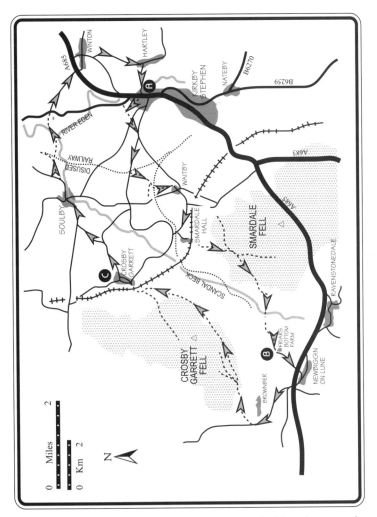

B - C Follow the road to meet the busy and fast A685 and go straight across into Newbiggin on Lune. At the T-junction by the converted church go R and meet the A685 again.

Jink L then immediate R, signed for Kelleth and Great Asby. Ignore the L and carry on, on this road, for Great Asby to pass Brownber Hall on the R. Climb past buildings, an electricity substation and a barn. The limestone pavements to the north come into view ahead of you. The road levels out and immediately after what appears to be the last field on the R you turn R off the road and onto a faint green track alongside the wall on the R. In about 400m bend R and briefly follow a very well surfaced vehicle track (to small reservoir). After the track ends stay near the wall on the R and head into the field corner ahead, by the barn. Through the gate the track soon divides into three. You should follow the bottom option to pass under a small rocky outcrop. CAUTION - Careful navigation now required. There are several branching bridleways but you will be following the correct line if you stay between the wall on your R and the line of hills on the L (first you pass Bents Hill, with a small cairn on its summit, then the long smooth profile of Nettle Hill). The long ridge of the north Pennines stretches out in front of you. About 3km after leaving the road you meet an excellently surfaced track by the wall on the R. Follow this on a great descent of about 2km, to enter Crosby Garrett under the Settle Carlise line.

C - A In Crosby Garrett the main village street divides into two, either side of a pretty beck. Follow down the R-hand side of the beck and climb to the beautifully positioned church. Bear R out of the village and stay on this road to a T-junction in about 1.5km. Go R and enter Soulby (look out for the remains of the old village pump on the R). At the crossroads go straight across, signed for Little Musgrave and Great Musgrave. Ignore the first bridleway on the R which goes straight across a ford and continue to the next L-hand bend. Head straight on, onto a good track, signed as a dead end and as a byroad to Winton. Ignore the first L turn and head straight on, to descend alongside the river. The track briefly narrows to a path. Cross the beautiful wooden bridge and head L onto the track at the other side. Meet the road and head straight across, following signs for Winton. After about 1.2km meet the A685 and go straight across into the village of Winton. Bend L and follow the main street to crossroads. Go R for Hartley and Quarry and pass the Bay Horse Inn to leave Winton. Ignore the first split R and just coming into Hartley go R, signed for Kirkby Stephen (straight on into Hartley will take you onto route 1, which passes through Hartley). Follow this road to enter Kirkby Stephen over a bridge and at the A685 go L back to the town centre.

5 CROSBY RAVENSWORTH FELL

Start Orton village centre   **Grid ref** 624084

Distance 24km / 15 miles

Time Allowed 2-3 hours   **Off road riding**   54%

Gradient Difficulty *Easy - **Moderate** - Difficult - Very Difficult*

Track Surface / Roads The tracks used over this well-drained limestone area are generally in good condition. The only exception is the track between Beaon Hill and Great Asby Scar; this is very clear in some places but virtually dissappears in others. Careful use of the direction tips plus the backup of a 1:25,000 map and compass are useful here.

OS Maps
1:50,000 Landranger 91 Appleby in Westmorland
1:25,000 Outdoor Leisure 19 Howgill Fells / Upper Eden Valley

Access There is no train link to Orton and, although the west coast main line passes near the village, there are no stations on it for many miles in either direction! Kirkby Stephen station on the Settle - Carlisle railway is some 19km / 12 miles away.

The track near Smardale Hall (ride 4)

ALONG THE WAY

• **Orton** Quiet Westmorland village sheltering beneath the steep slope of Orton Scar. Like many such villages its previous plethora of local services and tradesmen is now much reduced. Of the four inns only the **George Hotel** is still trading (bar meals available), and the post office doubles as the only store in the village. The two tearooms are a boon for daytrippers and those passing through, and one of them even doubles as a maker of fine chocolate! The village's more imposing buildings include Orton Hall and All Saints Church. In season it is a popular halt on the Coast to Coast walk.

• Highly unusual **limestone pavement** scenery awaits you on the crossing of Beacon Hill and Great Asby Scar. This is a highly environmentally sensitive landscape as well as a rare and eyecatching one (national nature reserve). In many places the limestone has weathered into regularly shaped square blocks covering many square miles of this upland area.

• **Crosby Ravensworth** is a gem of a village hidden in the Lyvennet Valley whose waters eventually join the Eden's near Temple Sowerby. A beautiful parish church dominates the main street and a beck with grassy banks completes the scene. Crosby Hall and Jennywell Hall are major buildings in the village which boasts a post office and the **Butchers Arms** pub.

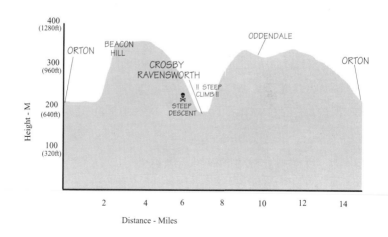

DIRECTIONS

A - B From the centre of Orton village head past the George Hotel on your R, following the B6260. After about 300m take the first L, signed for Gaisgill, Raisbeck and Kirkby Stephen to cross over the beck and head out of Orton. Head straight over the first crossroads out of the village signed for Raisbeck. Immediately past a roadside deciduous plantation take an unsigned track on the L that clearly climbs to the L of a limestone outcrop ahead of you. Part way along this track a bridleway to Acres, on the R, is the Coast to Coast walk, and leads through the same field as a stone circle. Ignore this bridleway and climb to a gate.

Through the gate bear L to pass between a wall on the L and a tiny, fenced off reservoir to the R, on the side of the limestone outcrop known as Knott. The rocky green track carries straight on into a very large enclosure as the wall drops away on the L. Pick up the line of the track as it heads diagonally and L towards the gate in the far L hand corner. Through the gate it is very easy to lose the track. Head diagonally L, just to the R of the cairn on Beacon Hill, to go through a gate in the wall (aim too far to the R and you will miss the wall completely and find yourself on the limestone of Great Asby Scar). Through the gate the bridleway continues straight ahead to cross a tarmac quarry road after about 500m following the very faint line of the bridleway. A smooth green surface improves for a few hundred metres after crossing straight over the tarmac road. Rising, single track takes over before disappearing altogether. Pick a line ahead and very slightly to your L, aiming for a small clump of trees by the B6260 road (traffic now reveals the line of this road although it is not entirely visible). Emerge at a T-junction formed by the B-road and a minor road. (Compass and 1:25,000 map advised).

B - C Go R at this T-junction and in about 600m go up a small rise and pass a quarry on the R. Turn L here following the broad, green byroad of Bank Lane. This broad green track descends gradually to pass Bank Head farm buildings on the R. Converging walls guide you onto a steep tarmac descent into Crosby Ravensworth, crossing Lyvennet Beck to come to a T-junction. Go L and bend R to pass the parish church on the R. Take the next R, signed for Shap, opposite the village hall. A steep climb takes you through a plantation. Pass the R turn for Wickerslack and the next R for Reagill. Go L onto the track signed as a bridleway to Oddendale. The initial enclosed section becomes a track over open pasture through a gate. Stay on the line of the track to pass under pylons. The M6 and a quarry reveal themselves on the R. Over the hill brow descend to a gate that leads to a grassy open space next to a minor road. Follow the road L as it bends L behind the farm settlement of Oddendale where it becomes a track.

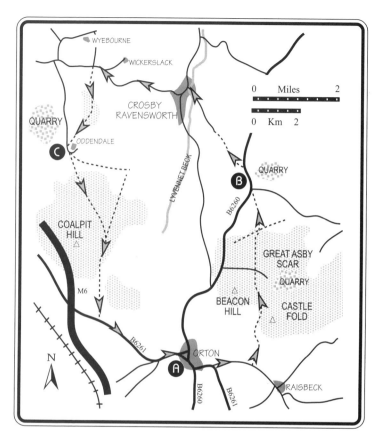

C - A Follow the main track as it bends R, away from the bank of trees behind Oddendale. Now on the open fell the track skirts a conifer plantation before briefly joining a wall on the R. This wall is soon left and the track passes another group of conifers down to the L. Climb to the brow ahead of you where another good quality track joins obliquely from the L and you stay on the established track. Ignore track junctions from hereon, maintaining your southerly direction on the main track. Eventually this track starts to descend, heading for telecommunications masts on the fells of southern Lakeland in the distance. Join the access track for Howe Nook on a bend and head R to the road. Go L onto the B6261 and follow it for about 3km back into Orton.

6 RUTTER FORCE / HIGH CUP GILL

Start Appleby train station   **Grid ref** 686207

Distance 43km / 27 miles (option omitting High Cup Gill is 34km / 21 miles)

Time Allowed 5 - 6 hours for the full route

Off road riding   45% for the full route, 25% for the shorter route

Gradient Difficulty *Easy - Moderate - **Difficult** - Very Difficult* (**Easy** for the shorter route)

Track Surface / Roads Although roads make up a large part of this route this is compensated for by the natural spectacles of Rutter Force and High Cup Gill. An excellent broad track leads to Rutter Force and a similarly good track leads part way up to High Cup Gill before the surface degenerates to a broad rocky path. The bridleway to Blacksyke Farm begins as good farm track before passing through a field to an exciting section of single track above a wood.

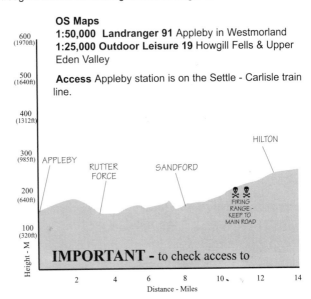

OS Maps
1:50,000 Landranger 91 Appleby in Westmorland
1:25,000 Outdoor Leisure 19 Howgill Fells & Upper Eden Valley

Access Appleby station is on the Settle - Carlisle train line.

HILTON

APPLEBY

RUTTER FORCE

SANDFORD

FIRING RANGE - KEEP TO MAIN ROAD

IMPORTANT - to check access to

Height - M

600 (1970ft)
500 (1640ft)
400 (1312ft)
300 (985ft)
200 (640ft)
100 (320ft)

Distance - Miles
2   4   6   8   10   12   14

ALONG THE WAY

• **Appleby in Westmorland** . Historic and picturesque market settlement set on a loop in the River Eden with many fine old buildings lining the main street, Boroughgate. The **Castle**, at the top end of Boroughgate, is based on a Norman fortification. Castle grounds, including Norman keep and the Rare Breeds Survival Trust, are open to the public (summer months). At the bottom of Boroughgate the tourist information office is housed in the old **Moot Hall** and further down, through The Cloisters, is the beautiful St. Lawrence's Church. Two unusual tall, white crosses at either end of Boroughgate mark the old sites of the cheese and butter markets. The annual Horse Fair in June attracts many travellers and even more tourists looking to photograph them!

• The **New Inn** at Hoff serves bar meals.

• **Rutter Force** is a lovely spot complete with footbridge, ford, mill building (now a gallery), cottage (now a cafe) and the low, wide waterfalls.

• **Sandford** Residential cum farming village with the large Sandford Arms at its centre, offering food and accommodation.

• **Cross Keys** pub is found on entering the tiny settlement of Hilton.

• **High Cup Gill** is surely one of the most dramatic valleys in the whole of England. The route leads part way along its northern edge, giving you plenty of opportunity to admire the great walls of volcanic Whin Sill rock and High Cup Nick itself, the dramatic apex of the elongated horseshoe shape of this deep glacial valley. BEWARE: the track used passes within a few feet of the very steep edge in places. Deteriorating path quality and use by Pennine Wayers mean the route goes only so far along the north lip before turning back. High Cup Gill is also an excellent 'there and back' route, starting in Appleby and going via Dufton.

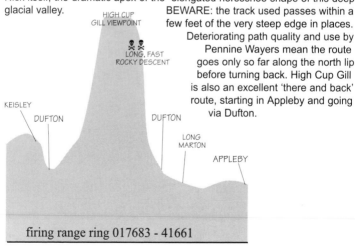

• **Dufton** is a charming village spread around a broad green. Being on the Pennine Way helps it support a post office, youth hostel, camping facilities and the **Stag Inn** (free house / food served)
• The **Masons Arms** in Long Marton serves food. Village store.

Under High Cup Nick (ride 6)

Right: East of Bassenthwaite (ride 11)
Below: The Howgills from Smardale
        Fell (ride 4)

Above: Descending from the Bewcastle Fells (ride 15)
Below: The track near Smardale Hall (ride 4)

Above: Looking down the Glenderaterra Valley (ride 11)
Below: Horse and Farrier Inn, Threlkeld (ride 11)

Above: Track near Swarthbeck (ride 10)
Below: Wandle Hill bridleway (ride 2)

DIRECTIONS

A - B Go R in front of Appleby station and immediate L in front of the Midland Hotel. R at the end of Clifford St and L at the next T-junction to descend to the B6542. L here then first R to cross the main bridge over the Eden. Bend L to go up Boroughgate and follow this road out of Appleby (B6260). Pass through Burrells and in Hoff go L signed for Drybeck. About 2km after this turning take a track on the L, signed 'Public Byway, Rutter Force'. This good quality track comes to a T-junction where you go L to descend to Rutter Force where you can use the bridge or ford. Climb away from Rutter Force on the tarmac and meet the road to go L. R at the next T-junction for Ormside and Soulby then L at the next crossroads for Ormside and Little Ormside. Just past Wild Rose Caravan Park turn R, signed 'Ormside, avoiding low bridge'. Under the Settle-Carlisle railway turn R over Helm Beck, with a choice of either stepping stones or ford, and through Ormside Mill follow this lovely tree-lined track to a track T-junction. Go L here and descend to farm buildings. Go R here and leave Little Ormside passing Terrys Farm on the L.

B - C Follow this farm track to a split, keeping R. The hedge lined track goes through a gate and through two fields. In the next field you lose the line of this track but follow the L edge with a large bank of woods sloping down to the Eden on your L. Through the gate in the corner descend on the single track to Blacksyke Farm (beware - farmer here very worried about hitting bikes with his tractor!). Through the farmyard go L to ascend on the road into Sandford.

Follow the road through the village, bending L by the Sandford Arms. At the T-junction with the B6259 go L under the old railway bridge to meet the A66 and go R (CAUTION - VERY FAST & BUSY). Take the next L signed for 'Entry no1 - ABC ranges'. Climb on this road into the military firing range. (STAY ON THE ROAD AND IGNORE ALL MINOR TURNINGS - SEE CONTACT NUMBER AT BEGINNING OF CHAPTER FOR RANGE ACCESS). Follow this road to a T-junction by the Cross Keys Inn and R through Hilton. At the T-junction over the beck go R for Murton and Dufton. Follow the road for another 6km through Murton and Keisley to descend to a T-junction and R.

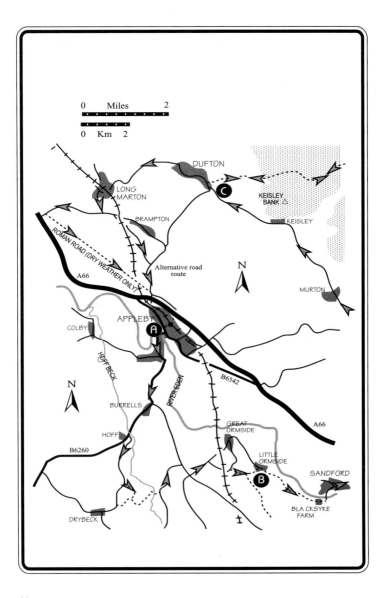

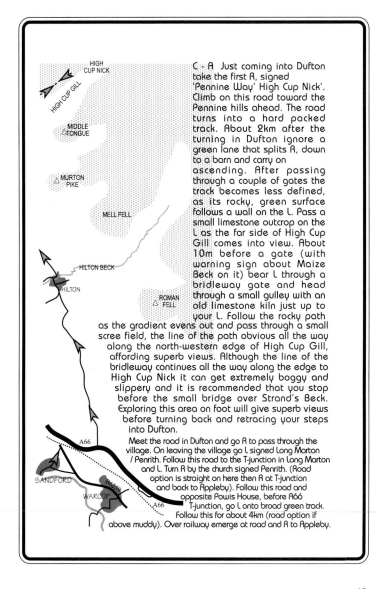

C - A Just coming into Dufton take the first R, signed 'Pennine Way' High Cup Nick'. Climb on this road toward the Pennine hills ahead. The road turns into a hard packed track. About 2km after the turning in Dufton ignore a green lane that splits R, down to a barn and carry on ascending. After passing through a couple of gates the track becomes less defined, as its rocky, green surface follows a wall on the L. Pass a small limestone outcrop on the L as the far side of High Cup Gill comes into view. About 10m before a gate (with warning sign about Maize Beck on it) bear L through a bridleway gate and head through a small gulley with an old limestone kiln just up to your L. Follow the rocky path as the gradient evens out and pass through a small scree field, the line of the path obvious all the way along the north-western edge of High Cup Gill, affording superb views. Although the line of the bridleway continues all the way along the edge to High Cup Nick it can get extremely boggy and slippery and it is recommended that you stop before the small bridge over Strand's Beck. Exploring this area on foot will give superb views before turning back and retracing your steps into Dufton.

Meet the road in Dufton and go R to pass through the village. On leaving the village go L signed Long Marton / Penrith. Follow this road to the T-junction in Long Marton and L. Turn R by the church signed Penrith. (Road option is straight on here then R at T-junction and back to Appleby). Follow this road and opposite Powis House, before A66 T-junction, go L onto broad green track. Follow this for about 4km (road option if above muddy). Over railway emerge at road and R to Appleby.

7 CROSS FELL CHALLENGE

Start Langwathby village centre   **Grid ref** 570337

Distance 55km / 34 miles   **Time Allowed** 8-9 hours

Off road riding   54%

Gradient Difficulty *Easy - Moderate - Difficult - **Very Difficult***

Track Surface / Roads Hellish gradients are the worst aspect of this ride - or the best if you really want a challenge to end all challenges! Although undoubtedly the most difficult ride in the book and very definitely only for the experienced and fit, this traverse of the very high northern Pennines contains panoramic vistas in the very truest sense of the word, taking in views of both the distant Lake District and vast tracts of Pennine Fells. Unavoidably, the A686 is used for several kilometres and care should be taken round the sharp bends; this is especially so on summer weekends when it is usually busy with motorbikers. The return leg passing near Cross Fell is about 90% rideable in the dry and features a superb green lane descent to Kirkland. **IMPORTANT NOTE - This route should not be attempted in anything but fine weather conditions and close reading of the large scale Outdoor Leisure map is advised.**

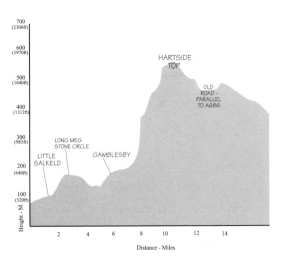

OS Maps
1:50,000 Landranger
> 90 Penrith & Keswick (contains the very start of the route only)
> 91 Appleby in Westmorland
> 86 Haltwhistle & Brampton

1:25,000 Outdoor Leisure
> 5 English Lakes North Eastern Area
> 31 Northern Pennines (small 'gap' in between maps)

Access Langwathby railway station is on the famed Settle-Carlisle line.

ALONG THE WAY

• **Langwathby** was originally a collection of 20 or so small farms but now it combines agriculture with its role as a commuter settlement for Penrith and Carlisle. The large and pretty village green is surrounded by a post office and store, church and **Shepherds Inn** pub which serves food. Cafe next to train station.
• **Little Salkeld** Just before entering the village proper look out for the water-powered mill producing organic flour which also has its own shop and cafe. Restricted opening times - for details phone 01768 881523. (Continued on page 50)

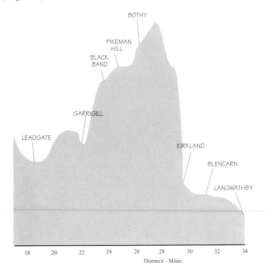

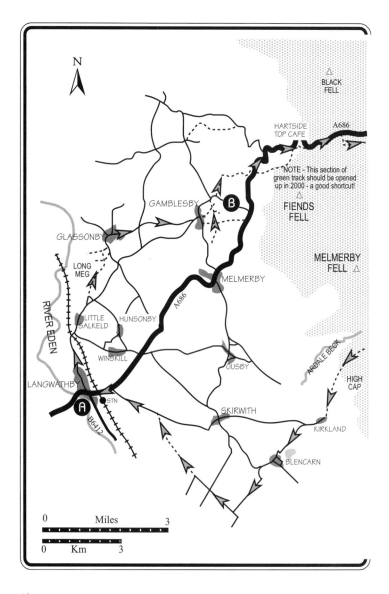

BLACK
FELL

HARTSIDE
TOP CAFE   A686

NOTE - This section of
green track should be opened
up in 2000 - a good shortcut!

GAMBLESBY   B

FIENDS
FELL

GLASSONBY

MELMERBY
FELL

LONG
MEG

MELMERBY

RIVER EDEN

A686

LITTLE
SALKELD   HUNSONBY

WINSKILL

ARDALE BECK

OUSBY

HIGH
CAP

LANGWATHBY

A   STN

B6412

SKIRWITH

KIRKLAND

BLENCARN

N

0   Miles   3
0   Km   3

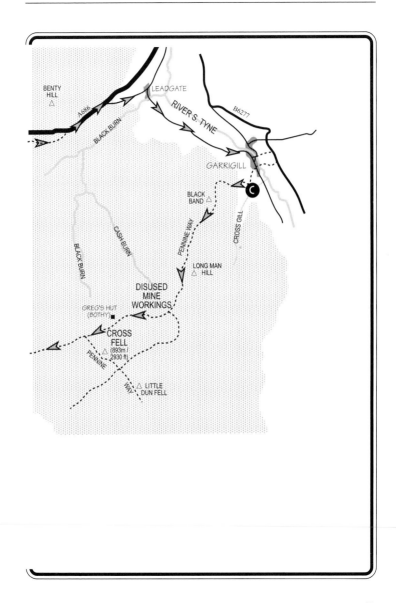

• **Long Meg and Her Daughters** Impressive prehistoric stone circle in a superb setting. 60 stones arranged in a layout with a 360 foot diameter. Their purpose is uncertain but they have possible funerary connections.
• **Hartside** 580m (1850ft) viewpoint across the Eden Valley and Lake District. Hartside Top cafe is a welcome break after the killer climb to this highpoint.
• **Garrigill** Small village grouped around a picturesque green and boasting a pub, tearoom, blacksmith's forge and waterfalls walk.
• **Cross Fell** The route passes near the summit of the highest mountain in England outside of the Lake District (893m / 2930ft). The peak can be seen from a distance as can the 'golfball' of the air traffic radar station on **Great Dun Fell**. However, close to, its peak is hidden by the sharp shoulders of scree slopes. The track we use over Cross Fell is known as the Old Corpse Road, possibly having been used by Garrigill folk to take their dead for burial in Kirkland!
• This ride uses sections of two long distance routes, the walkers' **Pennine Way**, from Garrigill to Cross Fell, and **Sustrans' C2C** bikers route, from Hartside to Garrigill. We saw far more cyclists than walkers when doing this route - a testimony to the current popularity of the C2C.

DIRECTIONS

A - B Start by the village green in Langwathby and head away from the village centre, passing St Peters Church on your R. Follow the road under the railway bridge and into Little Salkeld. About 0.25km out of Little Salkeld take the first L, just after the village sign. Bear L on meeting a tarmac road and carry straight on to meet Long Meg and Her Daughters stone circle. Head off the track and down the R-hand side of the stone circle, into the corner of the field. Go through the gate and down the R side of the next field. In the next field go down the L side to meet a conifer plantation, following the path to the L of this plantation. In the next field head down the L-hand side to cross over a farm road and across another field and into church grounds.

At the front of Addingham church bear R onto the road and at the first T-junction in about 150m go L and into Glassonby. Go R at the small grass triangle and R at the next T-junction for Gamblesby and Melmerby. Simply follow this road for about 3km to enter Gamblesby at the crossroads by the village stocks. Go R for Melmerby and Penrith. Opposite St Johns church go L up what appears to be the driveway of Church View. This byway becomes a stony track. Ignore the first track off to the R and at the first track crossroads go L. Keep on this track, ignoring any turnings off. At the road junction go immediate R, signed for Hazel Rigg and Alston. In about 200m go L and pass in front of the farm as the road becomes a stony track.

B - C This track bends R to climb very steeply as superb views unfold behind you, over the Eden Valley to the Lake District. About 2km after joining this track meet the A686 and L onto it (caution can be busy and fast at peak times). Follow the main road for about 3km to turn R onto a stony track, opposite a white building on the L. Climb steeply to the impressive viewpoint of Hartside Top and cafe. Go R back onto the A686. In about 1.25km, opposite an old disused house, go R onto the rough, unsigned track and descend, bending L.

Follow this walled track as it levels out and runs parallel to the A686 up to your L. Climb to rejoin the main road and R. Take the next R turn for Garrigill and Thortergill Force. Descend to the T-junction in Leadgate and R again. Climb and descend into Garrigill on this minor road. Stay down the R-hand side of the green and heading out of the village look for the track on the R signed as the Pennine Way. Past the Primitive Methodist Chapel (1885) on the L the track climbs fairly steeply and bends R then L onto the minor summit of Black Band.

NOTE You are now on a very exposed crossing of the high Pennines - take notice of the warning at the beginning of this ride.

C - A It is simply a case of following a largely well-defined track all the way to Kirkland. Cross Fell soon comes into view. Stay on the main track, ignoring any minor turnings. After about 4km Cash Burn reveals itself down to the R. Coming to disused mine workings the track ascends steeply - follow the main track as indicated by 'PW' on the small stone post. The stone cairn-like structures hide the entrance to deep mine shafts so beware. The track levels out again and aims for the Bothy known as Greg's Hut. Stay on the track past the bothy and the track climbs over the shoulder of Cross Fell (scree edge up to your L) losing its stony surface. The Pennine Way is soon signed off to the L. Ignore this and carry straight on, over the highest point on the ride. Soon a glorious view over the Eden Valley to the Lakes opens up and you begin to descend over very boggy terrain to join a stony track on a 90 degree bend.

Head L onto this. The initial surface is bouldery but soon turns into a glorious green lane descent into Kirkland with great views over Ardale Beck. Through Kirkland, by the bridge, go L for Blencarn. Pass the lake and in Blencarn go R at two successive T-junctions. Take the next L, just out of the village, signed for Newbiggin. Go R at the next T-junction and straight across the next crossroads. The road bends L but you carry straight on, onto a level track. Follow this for about 3km and L at the road T-junction at its end. L on meeting the A686 which descends into Langwathby.

Above: The track towards Cross Fell (ride 7)
Below: A quiet spot on Garrigill green (ride 7)
Opposite: The descent from Mohope Moor (ride 8)

8 SOUTH TYNE & WEST ALLEN VALLEYS

Start Alston town centre   **Grid ref** 717465

Distance 35km / 22 miles

Time Allowed 4.5 - 5.5 hours   **Off road riding** 46%

Gradient Difficulty *Easy - Moderate - **Difficult** - Very Difficult*

Track Surface / Roads Mainly good wide tracks with a stone base. The Ouston Fell track will get muddy but its good stone base should keep it rideable throughout the year. Descents off Ouston Fell and into Nenthead are rocky, steep and fast and care should be taken. The short byroad between Nether Harsley and Limestone Brae is perhaps the most difficult section combining steep gradients and deep ruts to cross a beautiful section of the River West Allen. Most roads in this isolated area are quiet although main roads around Alston will carry tourist traffic at peak weekends.

OS Maps
1:50,000 Landranger 86 Haltwhistle and Brampton
1:25,000 Outdoor Leisure 31 Northern Pennines

Access There are no train stations within striking distance of Alston but it lies handily on the crossroads of the A686 and A689 in the high Northern Pennines. You may be able to arrange for bike transport in the local area with Wrights buses of Nenthead (01434) 381200.

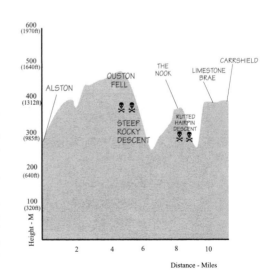

ALONG THE WAY

• **Alston** hides itself in the deep folds of the Pennines where the Nent valley joins that of the South Tyne. At 919ft this characterful settlement claims to be the highest town in England and was once the busy hub of a thriving Quaker-owned lead mining industry. During the nineteenth century it claimed 10,000 inhabitants, much more than today's population. The growing tourist industry has helped promote numerous tearooms, pubs and food shops and there is plentiful accommodation. Once a BR branch line joined Alston to the Haltwhistle. Now only 2.5 miles remains, operated in season as a visitor attraction.

• **The West Allen Valley**, dotted with tiny settlements such as Limestone Brae and Carrshields, is as beautiful as it is remote. A difficult byroad crosses the river below the former, then on joining the minor road you get spectacular views across this little visited corner of the northern Pennines.

• **Nenthead**, claiming to be England's highest village, is dour but interesting. A planned settlement for mineworkers, it allegedly has a colder climate than Aberdeen! Mineworkers could enjoy the benefits of a reading room, Methodist church and village hall. The **Mines Heritage Centre and Historic Site** is based on a former mining site and has a cafe. (01434) 382037. **Miners Arms** has meals and real ales.

• **Garrigill** Pretty village green with pub. Tearooms on the road out via Blacksmith's Forge and Waterfall Walk. Seasonal opening. (01434) 381936.

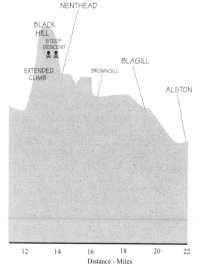

At the bridge over the
River West Allen (ride 8)

DIRECTIONS

A - B Start by the Town Hall in Alston and head down the cobbled Front Street to the T-junction. R onto the A686 signed for Hexham / Newcastle. On leaving Alston take the R turn onto CoatleyHill (North Loaning) and climb very steeply to a T-junction. Go L and on meeting the A686 go straight across onto a minor road signed for Ayle. Where the road bends 90 degrees L take a R turn by mine workings on the R. Immediately after a small plantation on the R go R up a track signed as a public byroad to Ninebanks and Long Cross. This climbs and bends L to meet the A686 again. Head straight across onto the driveway to Clargillhead (tearoom in season). Past the house on the R go through several gates as a good track leads through a plantation and then out onto Ouston Fell. Simply follow the track over the fell, eventually swinging L alongside a wall then through a sheep pen to descend a steep, rocky track to the road. Go L and descend steeply on the road to the River West Allen.

B - C Don't cross over the bridge but go R, signed for Middle and Farney Shield. Ignore the gated road to the R which goes to Helseywell Farm and carry on climbing above the West Allen Valley. Shortly, after a road joins obliquely from the R, turn L by The Nook to descend to Nether Harsley. Immediately before the farm buildings go R by the gate and descend to cross a brook then climb onto a grass track above the Allen Valley. Through a gate jink 90 degrees L down a rutted sunken lane to cross the River West Allen over a narrow bridge. Ascend the track to join a tarmac road and head R to ascend to a T-junction with a minor road.

Go R and through Limestone Brae climb gradually to a T-junction. Go R and pass through Carrshield. Follow this road for a further 5km or so up an extended climb that eventually passes through Coalcleugh and hairpins up to Black Hill, the highest point on the route. Just after passing out of Northumberland head R down an unsigned, wide rocky track (BEWARE - STEEP DESCENT. Control your speed). Meeting the road the route continues to the R (Nenthead village and its services are down to the L).

C - A On this minor road above the Nent valley pass Greenends and take the first R (unsigned) to pass Low Browngill. The road ends at a track split. Go L, signed as a public byroad to Blagill. Ignore the byroad turning L to Foreshield, following the track until it descends to the B6294. Go R and hairpin L into the hamlet of Blagill.

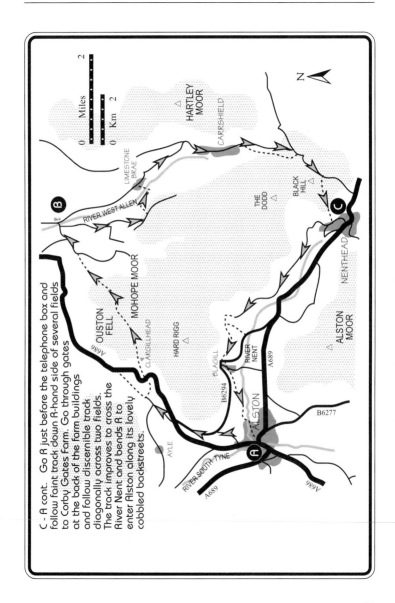

C - A cont.   Go R just before the telephone box and follow faint track down R-hand side of several fields to Corby Gates farm. Go through gates at the back of the farm buildings and follow discernible track diagonally across two fields. The track improves to cross the River Nent and bends R to enter Alston along its lovely cobbled backstreets.

9 GELTSDALE

Start Brampton railway station / town centre   **Grid ref** 874898

Distance 39km / 24miles (slightly shorter if beginning from Brampton train station)

Time Allowed 4-5 hours   **Off road riding** 41%

Gradient Difficulty *Easy - __Moderate__ - Difficult - Very Difficult*

Track Surface / Roads The centrepiece of this run is the outstanding Spelter Road. An excellent track climbs eastwards from Talkin Head farm to join this wild moorland crossing beneath Tarnmonath Fell. The excellent stone surface still appears in places from beneath a smooth green covering. The only tricky spot is the collapsed bridge across the River Gelt which requires a small, steepish scramble (WARNING - don't attempt this route in spate!). The road is a little overgrown either side of this former bridge but soon improves for a short but superb descent to Newbiggin. The return leg is largely on minor roads and the usually quiet B6413 before a beautiful bridleway crossing of the River Gelt. The section of track under Tarnmonath Fell is shown as a footpath on OS maps but this is widely accepted as an error of judgement and will hopefully be rectified in future.

OS Maps
1:50,000 Landranger 86 Haltwhistle & Brampton
1:25,000 Outdoor Leisure
43 Hadrians Wall

Access Brampton train station is on the Carlisle - Newcastle line and is 1.5 miles from the town centre. Directions are given from both the town centre and the station.

ALONG THE WAY

• **Brampton** originated as a market town with further development in the 18th century from mining and the building of the Newcastle-Carlisle Military Road. Today the attractive Market Place is dominated by the unusual Moot Hall housing the tourist information office / council chamber and Front Street is lined with a wide variety of pubs and shops. The Mote is probably the remnants of an old Norman castle and is good viewpoint. Town architecture includes several Methodist buildings and St Martin's Church.

• **Talkin** boasts the **Blacksmiths Arms** (food/accommodation) and **Hare & Hounds** (food) pubs.

• **Spelter Road** Once the primary route used by zinc refiners based at Tindale at the northern end of the route. Carts full of ore were bought from as far away as the Isle of Man for refining here. The refined metal was then taken back along the same track. The remains of the collapsed bridge hint at a very substantial structure capable of taking very heavy carts.

• Much of Geltsdale and the surrounding countryside is designated as an **SSSI (Site of Special Scientific Interest)** and has several other protection classifications which aim to protect the unusual wildlife here (mainly moorland birds). Under no circumstances should you stray from the clear line of the path; please heed this warning and protect this fragile and rare ecosystem.

• **Newbiggin** Tiny settlement nestling on the western edge of the Pennines. **Blue Bell Inn** does meals most evenings and weekend lunchtimes.

• **Castle Carrock** Distinguished looking village. **Weary Sportsman** and **Duke of Cumberland** pubs. The former has food and accommodation.

• **Talkin Tarn Country Park** Country Park with boating and fishing activities and a tearoom. **Tarn End Hotel** nearby is open to non-residents and serves bar meals plus tea and coffee.

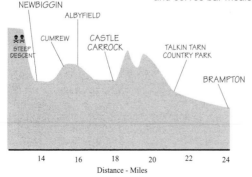

NEWBIGGIN
ALBYFIELD
STEEP DESCENT
CUMREW
CASTLE CARROCK
TALKIN TARN COUNTRY PARK
BRAMPTON

14   16   18   20   22   24

Distance - Miles

DIRECTIONS   **Please be sure to shut all gates on this route!**

A - B If starting in Brampton centre face the front of the tourist information centre and head up the R hand side, onto Craw Hall (B6413). Pass Brampton Old Brewery Development and leave Brampton to pass under the main A69. Take the next L turn for Brampton Junction and Hallbankgate. Pass over the railway and pass the station on the L. If joining the route here by train exit from the south platform and L (the platform without the large wooden shelter). At the next T-junction (unsigned) go R and at the next T-junction to go R for Farlam, Talkin and Castle Carrock. Pass through Farlam and climb into Talkin. Go L at the crossroads by the Blacksmiths Arms, signed for Forest Head. On the edge of the village turn R signed for Talkin Head 1/2. Descend past Talkin Head on the R where the tarmac becomes a rough track on crossing a beck. The track climbs steadily to reveal a lovely view over Geltsdale. Part way along a bridleway joins on the R, from Hynam Bridge. Cairns on the summit of Talkin Fell come into view up to your L and the track levels out and becomes grassier through a gate. Follow a wall on your L and immediately through a second gate bear R to follow a wall on your R, along the flat grassy track. Pass 'The Greens', a solitary house, and carry straight on as the wall angles away on your R. The clear track bends gradually L and hairpins down and R to cross How Gill at the disused building 'Gairs'.

B - C After 'Gairs' the track climbs steeply for about 200m to meet a track T-junction. Go R onto this track which runs almost level along the side of Tarnmonath Fell with superb views up Geltsdale. Simply follow the clear line of the Spelter Road and as Old Water comes into view beneath you the line of the track is apparent on the other side of the small valley. Zig-zag down to what appears to be a new bridge across Old Water. Over the bridge ignore the track that splits off R and follows the southern bank of the Gelt. The track deteriorates approaching a missing bridge over the river; a difficult scramble takes you over the river and onto the narrow path at the far side. This becomes rideable shortly and gradually improves to pass shooting boxes. A superb view opens up over northern Lakeland before a steep windy and rocky descent on an excellent track.

Descend to the T-junction in Newbiggin and R onto the minor road. At the T-junction with the B6413 go R for Castle Carrock and Brampton. Take the first R turn and bend L into the quiet settlement of Cumrew. As the road bends L turn R onto a very minor road. Ignore the track that bends to the R and stay on the tarmac, passing through a series of gates to farm buildings at Albyfield. Don't go into the farmyard but turn L and meet the B road again at another T-junction. Go R and follow the road for about 1.5 miles into Castle Carrock.

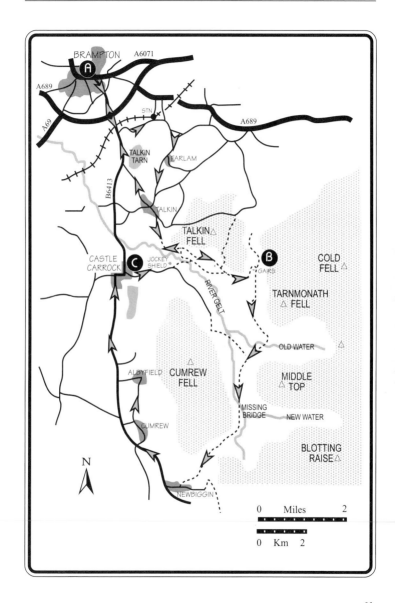

C - A In Castle Carrock bend R into the village centre then turn R to pass between The Weary Sportsman and the Duke of Cumberland Inns. Follow this road out of the village for about 2/3 of a mile and on a R-hand bend turn L down a gravel track marked as a private road (Jockey Shield). This descends to cross the River Gelt, with its rocky bed overhung by an arch of trees. Immediately over the bridge go L at the T-junction and follow the track to bend R in front of Low Hynam and climb steeply on this bridlepath to emerge at the track used on the original ascent to 'Gairs'. Go L onto it and descend to Talkin Head where you join the road.

You can now follow your outward route back to the start. Alternatively, to visit Talkin Tarn Country Park go straight across at the crossroads in Talkin to pass the Hare & Hounds on the L. This road descends past a great viewpoint over the tarn to a T-junction with the B6413. R here will take you back into Brampton via the main entrance to the Country Park.

Heading across Barton Fell (ride 10)

The descent after Swarthbeck Gill (ride 10)

10 AROUND ULLSWATER

Start Penrith train station   **Grid ref** 512299

Distance 40km / 25 miles (24km / 15 miles starting in Askham or Pooley Bridge)

Time Allowed 4-5 hours   **Off road riding**   40% (nearer 60% for the shorter version from Askham or Pooley Bridge).

Gradient Difficulty *Easy - **Moderate** - Difficult - Very Difficult*

Track Surface / Roads The bridleway starting by Heughscar Hill as the course of a Roman road and running for several miles down to Howtown is very well-defined and well-used, no doubt because of the superlative views of the mountain ranges towering behind the lake. Boggy, eroded areas are more of a problem the further into winter you go, so try and pick conditions when the ground will be hard. The Pooley Bridge - Helton bridleway has a much better, rockier surface. The A6 / B5320 link from Penrith is far from ideal because of heavy traffic but no viable off-road links existed at the time of writing. Those not relying on the train would be well-advised to start and finish in Askham or Pooley Bridge, cutting out 10 miles of less interesting road work.

OS Maps
1:50,000 Landranger 90 Penrith & Keswick
1:25,000 Outdoor Leisure 5. The English Lakes - North Eastern area.

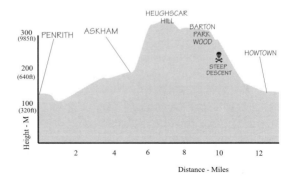

Access Penrith railway station is on the West Coast main line but the Settle - Carlisle line also runs close to Penrith (Langwathby station is about 8km / 5 miles east of the town centre on the C2C route).

ALONG THE WAY

• **Penrith** Red sandstone market town, based around a series of market places connected by narrow streets (a layout that was originally a defence against marauding Scots). The Castle, begun in the 14th century, was occupied by Richard of Gloucester as 'Guardian of the West March towards Scotland'. St Andrews Church is surrounded by the fine architecture of Bishop's Yard. Churchyard has 'Giant's Grave' (arrangement of ancient crosses and hogback graves) near Gothic monument to Robert Virtue (railway engineer). The central Musgrave Monument dates from 1851 and commemorates the early death of Lord and Lady Musgrave's son.

• **Askham** Not only a beautiful village but a beautifully kept one. Askham Hall is an Elizabethan mansion based around a fourteenth century defensive pele tower. St Peters church sits in a lovely spot by the River Lowther. **Punch Bowl Inn** and the **Queens Head** both serve food.

• This ride gives commanding views over **Ullswater**. The Lake District's second largest lake, it is generally much quieter than its largest, Windermere. Boating is still fairly popular and motor launches provide transport between **Pooley Bridge** and Glenridding. The former sits at the north-eastern end of the lake and, though small, boasts several shops, three pubs and a tourist information centre.

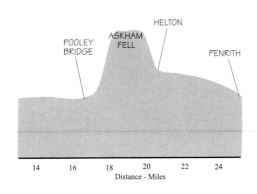

DIRECTIONS

A - B Head L infront of Penrith train station to the roundabout by
the castle and head down Castlegate (one way so wheel your bike
down the pavement) into Great Dockray. Follow Princes St then
Southend Rd, past the post office buildings, to come to a small
roundabout with the A6. Go R here and head out of Penrith. Caution
as the A6 crosses the A66 on a very busy roundabout. Straight over
the roundabout the road descends and climbs through Eamont Bridge.
Just out of Eamont Bridge take the R signed B5320 for Tirril and
Pooley. Just over the railway bridge at Yanwath go L, signed for
Askham and Haweswater. In about 3.5km, just before entering
Askham, take the R turn signed for Celleron and climb on this minor
road. In about 1.5km go L onto a bridleway, following the entrance
drive to High Winder House (self catering cottages).

B - C About 60m before the cottages ahead of you bear R onto
a very roughly defined grass track, over the field to pass through
a gate with a blue bridleway arrow on it. Climb on the rough track
under the telegraph wires slightly ahead and to the R. As you round
the corner of Heughscar Hill and bend L a superb vista over Ullswater
comes into view. Follow the track under the rock outcrop of Heughscar
Hill (muddy in places), ignoring a R hand downhill option. Continue
climbing and just over the brow of the hill fork R to drop down to
a sizeable cairn with a bridleway sign next to it. Cross straight over the
Pooley Bridge - Helton bridleway, following signs for Howtown and
Roman Road. Follow the well-defined track across a small beck
to the Cockpit stone circle on your L. Bear R at the track split here
onto the more major, stony track and over another small beck.

Follow the track as it aims for a point beneath White Knott crag and
Barton Park Woods. Cross over the steep sided Alk Beck and follow
the track alongside the wall at the top of Barton Park Woods. The
line of the track is clear for the next 4km or so, as it descends past
the spectacular crags of Swarthbeck Gill to eventually reach a gate
at Melguards. Bear L off the access drive, onto a green lane marked
as a bridleway. Just over Fusedale Beck, at the base of lonely
Fusedale up to your L, meet a road and R to descend into Howtown.
Split R in Howtown to meet the minor road that hugs the southern
coast of Ullswater. Go R on this road and follow the water's edge for
6km to the crossroads on the edge of Pooley Bridge. To visit Pooley
Bridge go L then L at the next roundabout. Otherwise head R at this
crossroads to start on the return route.

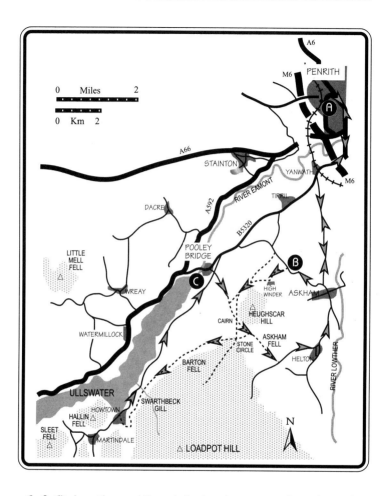

C - A Climb on the road through Roehead to a gate where the track
across Askham Fells starts. Simply stay on the track straight ahead, to
climb past the cairn on the R, and in about 3km meet a road. Go L
into Helton and bear L into Askham. Follow your outward route back
into Penrith by bearing L in front of the Queens Head pub.

11 AROUND SKIDDAW

Start Keswick town centre

Grid ref 266235

Distance 33km / 20.5 miles

Time Allowed 5-6 hours

Off road riding   63%

Gradient Difficulty *Easy - Moderate - **Difficult** - Very Difficult*

Track Surface / Roads Mainly good quality mountain tracks that are excellent in dry conditions. Forestry roads are used over the side of Latrigg, a steep but spectacular climb. Heading towards Skiddaw, a tarmac farm drive becomes a steepening rocky track leading to Whitewater Dash waterfall will need some pushing from all but aspiring supermen / women! Although of variable quality the whole of the track from here until rejoining the road near the Blencathra centre is rideable after dry conditions, and the last section is superb quality with equally superb views. The only heavy traffic likely to be encountered is where the route touches the A591 to the west of Bassenthwaite Lake.

OS Maps
1:50,000 Landranger 90 Penrith & Keswick (contains the very start of the route only)

Access There is no railway station at Keswick although there are large pay & display car parks in the centre. Keswick itself can get very busy at peak times.

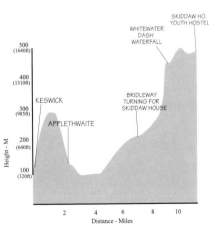

ALONG THE WAY

• **Keswick** Tourist and outdoor centre for the northern Lakes. Busy Main St. with interesting Moot Hall housing tourist information centre. Beautiful strolls in parks and by Derwentwater.
• **Dodd Wood** Forest Enterprise woods covering Dodd summit.
• **Skiddaw** peak towers over you for much of the ride, peaking at 931m or 3054ft above sea level.
• **Threlkeld** A choice of two pubs awaits in this small village nestling at the foot of Blencathra. Village activity was based on farming and quarrying until a tuberculosis sanatorium (now Blencathra study centre) was added in the late 19th century.
• **Keswick Railway Path** Once a major rail artery running west - east through the Lakes, from Workington to Penrith. The section used here is a specially surfaced cycle and walkway alongside some beautiful stretches of the River Greta and forms part of the C2C bike route. This climbs and drops to pass next to then under the main A66 before returning to the heart of Keswick.

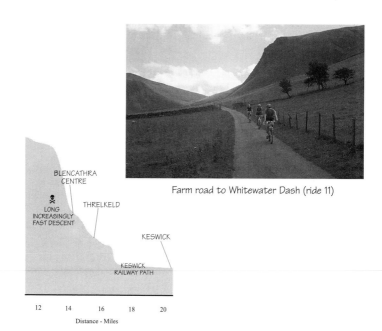

Farm road to Whitewater Dash (ride 11)

BLENCATHRA
CENTRE

LONG
INCREASINGLY
FAST DESCENT

THRELKELD

KESWICK

KESWICK
RAILWAY PATH

12   14   16   18   20

Distance - Miles

DIRECTIONS

A - B From Keswick centre head up Bank St then Victoria St and turn L onto Station Road with Upper Fitz Park on your R. As soon as you turn R onto Brundholme Road go L onto the C2C path link and pass the swimming pool. Pass the end of Keswick Rail Path and head to the mini-roundabout. Go L here, back onto Brundholme Rd. Take the first R up Spoony Green Lane bridleway. Pass over the bypass and start to climb on a steepening track past woods on the R. Great views unfold of the peaks behind Keswick and of Bassenthwaite Lake. Stay on the main track, ignoring minor turnings. The track levels out to pass mixed woodland on your L. About 2.5km after joining this track exit into the car park area and L onto the road (many bikers and walkers start routes from this car park).

Descend steeply to a T-junction in Applethwaite and R. Pass Crosthwaite Church and go through Millbeck, staying on this road to meet the A591 road (busy and fast). Go R onto this road. Pass Mirehouse car park by the main A591. Take the next R turn signed for Orthwaite and climb on this minor road. The road dips then rises steeply over Chapel Beck. About 3km after joining this minor road go R onto the tarmac road, through agate, signed as a bridleway to Skiddaw and Threlkeld via Dash Falls. Follow the tarmac road until a track splits off to the R, which you follow to climb steeply to pass next to Whitewater Dash Waterfalls.

B - A The track levels out and over the horizon Skiddaw towers up to your R. The rocky track descends then climbs to Skiddaw House Youth Hostel. At the hostel jink L then R to carry on in a south-easterly direction (the bridleway that heads north-east here runs alongside the Caldew to emerge at Mosedale). Cross the small bridge at Salehow Beck before superb views down the Glenderaterra Valley. Split L at the first opportunity and descend to cross Glenderaterra Beck. This superb shelf-like track heads along the east side of the valley to join a road through a car park area, by the Blencathra Centre. Descend into Threlkeld and at the T-junction at the end of Blease Road go R (pubs down to the L). Follow this road until heading onto the shared pedestrian / cycle path just before the major junction with the A66. This joins the Keswick Railpath and in 5km or so you emerge by Keswick pool.

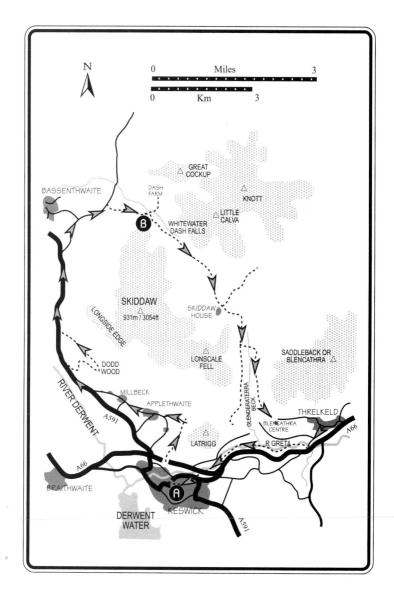

12 KESWICK - LORTON VALE

Start Keswick (route also accessible from Cockermouth)   **Grid ref** 263235

Distance 39km / 24 miles   **Time Allowed** 5-6 hours

Off road riding 29 %

Gradient Difficulty *Easy - __Moderate__ - Difficult - Very Difficult*

Track Surface / Roads Don't be put off by the relatively small amount of off-road content in this ride. The off-road sections that are used all give superb and varied views, and some of the minor roads used are extremely minor; the minor road before Ling Fell has so much grass and gravel on it that it amounts to a virtually off-road experience in many places and we encountered neither cars nor people when riding it. Extensive use is made of forestry roads through Whinlatter Forest Park and Wythop Woods. The descent through the latter is extremely steep and contains a lethal right hand hairpin.

OS Maps
1:50,000 Landranger 89 West Cumbria
1:25,000 Outdoor Leisure 4 English Lakes North Western Area

Access
There is no rail access into the northern Lake District; Keswick is roughly midway between Penrith and Workington railway stations (approximately 20 miles from each). The direction tips tell you how to join the route from Cockermouth which is only about 9 miles from Workington station on the Cumbria coastal line.

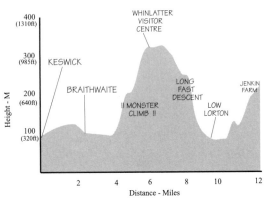

ALONG THE WAY

• **Keswick** Mecca for outdoor activities of all kinds including walking, climbing and mountain biking although note the centre can suffer from congestion at peak holiday times; not surprising as it is the main holiday centre for the northern Lakes. The interesting looking **Moot Hall** houses the tourist information centre and is found on Market Street. The **Pencil Museum** and **Cars of the Stars** are off-beat and interesting. The centre has possibly the greatest concentration of outdoor equipment shops per square metre anywhere in the world!
• **Braithwaite** Small, pretty village on Coledale Beck with handy collection of shops including village stores and two Jennings pubs, both serving food (small cycle spare outlet next to village store).

Resting at Whinlatter Visitor Centre (ride 12)

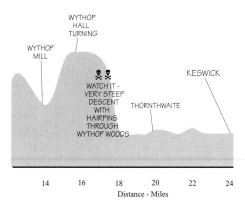

WYTHOP
HALL
TURNING

WYTHOP
MILL

WATCH IT -
VERY STEEP
DESCENT
WITH
HAIRPINS
THROUGH
WYTHOP WOODS

THORNTHWAITE

KESWICK

14   16   18   20   22   24

Distance - Miles

• Ascending the **Whinlatter Pass** gives you great views towards **Skiddaw** and its surrounding peaks. The visitor centre has a gift shop and cafe - a handy refreshment stop after the extremely steep and extended climbs from Thornthwaite. There are equally spectacular views to the east, coming over the pass. The flat bottom of **Lorton Vale** houses the River Cocker and beyond the **Solway Firth** appears, backed by the hills of Dumfries.
• There are also spectacular views from the sides of Long and Ling Fells, north towards **Cockermouth** and **Watch Hill**. The 'Gem Town' of Cockermouth is well worth a visit. It's easily reached along a spur of the C2C (see directions). For more detail on the town see page 79.
• Just when you thought the views couldn't get any better the descent through Wythop Woods reveals a stunning vista over **Bassenthwaite Lake** backed by Skiddaw. The Black Swan Hotel, just before you re-enter Thornthwaite serves food in the public bar. The white 'Bishop' rock opposite is painted yearly by the landlord.

Whinlatter Forest (ride 12)

Whinlatter Forest (ride 12)

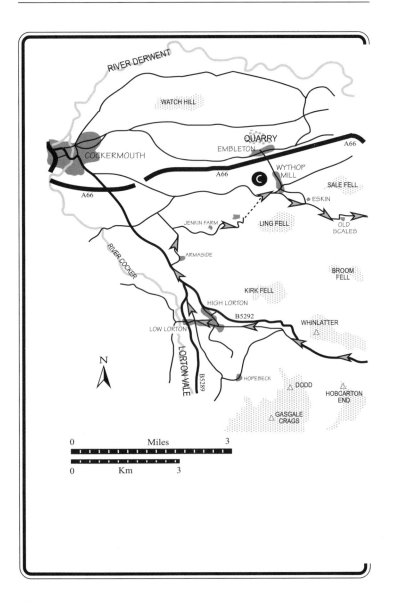

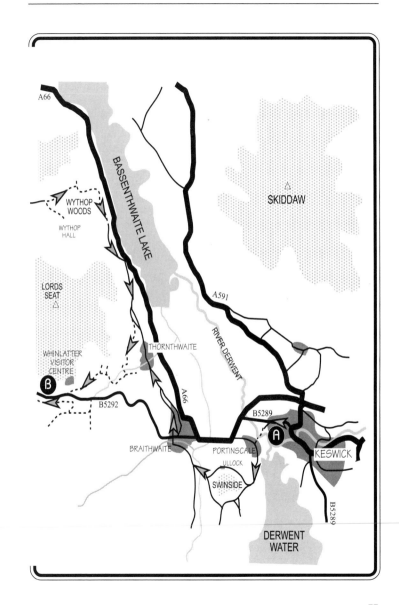

DIRECTIONS

A - B Head out of Keswick centre on Main Street, in a north-westerly direction, crossing over the River Greta. Turn L off this busy road, having left the buildings of Keswick behind you. The road is marked as a dead end but you can push your bike over the footbridge and rejoin a road at the other side to come into Portinscale. At the T-junction go L and take the next R turn which will take you round the north side of the conifer-covered hill of Swinside. Bear R at the next two junctions and into the pretty village of Braithwaite. Stay on the road to cross the beck and come to a crossroads by the Royal Oak pub. Head straight over and climb then drop to pass through Lanefoot Farm about 1km after Braithwaite.

At the next T-junction go L to come into Thornthwaite. Past the garage on the L take the next L, up a small tarmac road. After about 80m take the L turn steeply up the hill onto the gravel forestry road. After about 1km of steep climbing pass over Comb Beck and hairpin L and R bringing you to a T-junction. Go R and recross the beck. Stay on this main track, ignoring minor turnings off to the L then R. At the next T-junction follow signs for the visitor centre. Pass the visitor centre on the R to come to the B5292 road.

B - C Go L on the road and in about 200-300m go R by the Revelin Moss sign. Take the first R turn down the forest track before reaching the car park. Take the first R turn and after a small climb the track starts to descend parallel to the B-road down to the R with great views of the side of Whinlatter peak. Descend to a fork and go R to the car park next to the B-road. Go L onto the B-road and in just less than 1km go L onto a minor road for 'Hopebeck' and 'Narrow Gated Road'. Superb views open up before you; simply stay on this road to cross over a tiny beck to come to a T-junction in High Lorton.

Go L here to pass the school then post office to come to a staggered crossroads. Go R, signed 'Cockermouth 4'. Pass the church on the L and meet the B5289, going R for Cockermouth. The B5292 joins from the R but you carry on to take the next unsigned R (easy to miss). Pass through High Armaside and after passing Harrot Hill Farm take the next unsigned R. This climbs past Jenkin Farm and great views unfold to the north. About 1.5km after this farm the very minor road ends by farm buildings and is replaced by a steep rocky track which you follow. The track improves and levels out then descends to a T-junction with a minor road. Go R and on meeting the village sign for Wythop Mill turn R and climb steeply. You can glimpse the northern end of Bassenthwaite Lake from this road.

C - A   * Follow this road until it bends 90 degrees L just after Burthwaite Cottage. Turn R here, passing Eskin Farm on the L. The road bends through Old Scales Farm. The road ends and a track bends to Wythop Hall. Ignore this and go through the gate ahead to follow a lovely track over this green upland plateau. In about 3/4 of a kilometre head R where the track meets a gate and descend into Wythop Woods (follow C2C signs). The track narrows and steepens - BEWARE ROCKY SURFACE AND DROPS. At a hairpin there is a superb view over Bassenthwaite Lake. Meet a more major track running across your path. Turn R then immediate L to continue descending on a more minor track. The descent then bends R and becomes less severe. Emerge at the end of a road and head R and through a bus-turning circle following what is in fact the line of the old main road. Come to a T-junction with the A66 just on the L. Go R and in about 1km pass the Swan Hotel on the L. Pass through Thornthwaite and just leaving the village go R and through Lanefoot Farm. You can now retrace your outward steps through Braithwaite, Ullock and Portinscale back into Keswick.

* Note that the Cockermouth link joins just before Wythop Mill, where you emerged onto the road. From Cockermouth centre it is simply a matter of following C2C signs in an easterly direction to take the R turn when you see the sign for Wythop Mill. You can then pick up the directions at C - A above. Also see route 13.

Near Dash Farm (ride 11)

13 COCKERMOUTH TO DUBWATH

Start Cockermouth town centre   **Grid ref** 123307

Distance 25km / 15.5 miles

Time Allowed 2 - 3 hours   **Off road riding**   44%

Gradient Difficulty *Easy - **Moderate** - Difficult - Very Difficult*

Track Surface / Roads Your outward route, via Wythop Mill to Dubwath, is largely on very minor roads. The return leg uses two fine, long off-road stretches, first dipping alongside the River Derwent then rising to the superb vantage point of Watch Hill. You should be aware that the first section alongside the river can be very muddy after rain and in winter. You ascend Watch Hill on an excellent track then drop down towards Cockermouth on a fairly well-defined grassy track through fields.

OS Maps
1:50,000 Landranger 89 West Cumbria
1:25,000 Outdoor Leisure 4 English Lakes North Western Area

Access There is no train line to Cockermouth, the nearest station being Workington, some 15km away on the Cumbrian coastal line.

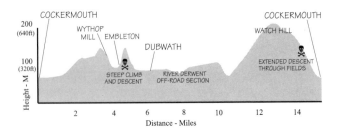

ALONG THE WAY

• **Cockermouth** A 'gem town' with many fine old buildings lining the wide main street and Castlegate. The **Norman Castle** on Castlegate is only occasionally open to the public. **Wordsworth House**, former residence of William and Dorothy Wordsworth, is now owned by the National Trust (admission fee for non-members). Other attractions include **Printing House Museum**, **Jennings Brewery Tour**, **Toy & Model Museum** and **All Saints Church.**
• There are excellent views over **Bassenthwaite Lake** from much of the route, backed by the Skiddaw range of mountains; this short moderate route is a good way to get close to this towering scenery whilst avoiding some of the more extreme tracks in the area.
• **Embleton** has the **Derwent Lodge Country House Hotel** and the **Wheatsheaf** (Jennings ales and bar meals).
• **Bassenthwaite village** lies just off the eastern end of the route. It is clustered at the base of the Skiddaw range, the Sun and Castle Inns making it a handy half way break.

Cockermouth's grand architecture (ride 13)

DIRECTIONS

A - B From the statue of R. Mayo, on Main Street in Cockermouth, head away from the statue in the direction it is facing. Turn R off Main Street down the side of the Globe Hotel, onto Challoner Street. (You are on the C2C route until Wythop Mill). L at the T-junction at the end of Challoner Street then R up Rubbybanks Road, alongside the River Cocker on the L. Continue under the road bridge, on the track. Under the next bridge follow C2C signs up a path and split R past a small row of houses on the R. Head R onto the bridge you have just passed under, now on the Greenway, a former rail trackbed. Stay on the main track, cross a tarmac road and pass the cemetery. Hairpin R, round the edge of the cemetery to the road opposite Strawberry How Business Centre.

Turn L and follow the road over the main A66. About 2.5km after joining the road go L at the first T-junction, signed Embleton and Keswick. Stay on this road, following signs for Wythop Mill. Just on entering Wythop Mill you leave the C2C, which climbs steeply up a R turn. In the centre of Wythop Mill go over the bridge and L at the crossroads, signed for Embleton. Descend to the A66 and straight across. Climb to the T-junction in Embleton and R.

Just out of Embleton turn L at Close Farm (easy to miss) and climb steeply on the narrow tarmac. Just as the climb levels out go R onto a track marked 'Unsuitable for Wide Vehicles'. Descend to a T-junction and R and in about 50m come to another T-junction. L here and just before meeting the T-junction with the A66 turn L onto the B5291, signed for Castle Inn. This road leads round the head of Bassenthwaite Lake, to a T-junction.

B - A Go R, signed Castle Inn, Bothel and Carlisle, to cross over the River Derwent as it enters the lake. In about 1km, on a R-hand bend, go L, immediately after the entrance to the Armathwaite Hall Hotel, marked as a dead end. Pass Coalbeck Farm and at the R-hand bend ignore the footpath signed to the R, carrying straight on, onto the rough bridleway to Isel (NOTE - can be very muddy in wet conditions). Descend alongside the River Derwent and through a gate pass Isel Old Park Wood on the R. Climb to join tarmac through Long Close Farm then meet a T-junction. Go L and descend for about 1km to another T-junction. L over the Derwent and climb to next T-junction where you go R for Cockermouth.

B - A(cont.) In about 250m go L onto a well-surfaced bridleway, skirting the bottom of a plantation. Ignore the first split L. After about 2km of ascent the track appears to hairpin back into the woods; here head through a gate on the R, and onto the grassy track down the R-hand side of a large field. Now on the grassy summit of Watch Hill, continue downhill on the grass track with superb views down Lorton Vale. Keep on the line of this track as it descends through several fields, and after about 1.5km of descent bend L to meet the road. R onto the road and simply avoid any turnings as you come into Cockermouth to descend back to Main Street.

83

14 THE CALDEW VALLEY

Start Dalston village centre

Grid ref 369501

Distance 27km / 17 miles

Time Allowed 4-5 hours

Off road riding 55%

Gradient Difficulty *Easy - __Moderate__ - Difficult - Very Difficult*

Track Surface / Roads Predominantly good tracks characterise this lovely route around the Caldew Valley. The Buckabank - Gaitsgill track is a little bumpy and prone to nettles in the summer but this is not a major problem. The excellent track away from Thistlewood Farm leads to an easy and rideable field section. The only other field section, from Hawksdale Hall to Bridge End, follows a well-defined, firm farm track. After Churchtown the route follows an off-road section of the long distance Reivers route and so all the tracks are of a reasonable quality (but beware the carry up short steps and over the footbridge at Bog Bridge after descending from Borrans Hill). All minor roads used are very quiet.

OS Maps
1:50,000 Landranger 85 Carlisle and Solway Firth

Access The railway station at Dalston is on the Cumbrian coastal line between Carlisle and Barrow in Furness. You may have to hail the train if returning by rail from Dalston. At the time of writing there were around 15 trains stopping daily at Dalston, Monday to Friday, but only 3 a day on Sundays!

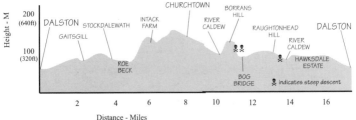

ALONG THE WAY

• **Dalston** is now a compact village but during the industrial revolution it possessed four cotton mills and a flax mill. The heart of the village is the square, surrounded by the church, the Bluebell Inn (food), a cafe and village shop. It is well worth stocking up on snacks here as there are no food outlets directly on the route.
• **Sebergham** and **Churchtown** once had a greater joint population than Penrith but today they are little more than hamlets.
• The **River Caldew** provides much of the scenic interest on this ride, along with its tributary, Roe Beck. The Caldew starts life high up in the Skiddaw region of the Lake District and flows south through this lovely wooded, rolling countryside before passing through Carlisle to join the Eden. There are many scenic highlights by the river, such as Bog Bridge after the descent from Borrans Hill. The distant outline of the **Caldbeck and Uldale** Fells is a frequent companion on this ride whilst the stunning green pasture in front of **Hawksdale Hall** provides a fitting climax to the trip.

Bog Bridge (ride 14)

DIRECTIONS

A - B Start in Dalston centre by the church and Bluebell Inn. Head south, away from the church, on the B5299. In about 60m, opposite the service station, go L, marked as a dead end for cars. Immediately over the River Caldew turn R to come alongside a small watercourse on the R. Follow this tarmac track past the chimney and workings to a T-junction. Go L to immediately come to another T-junction and L again to start climbing. Take the next R, signed 'Gaitsgill 2¼, Raughtonhead 3¼'. Take the first turning on the R, an unmarked minor road which ends at a track junction with Brackenhow Farm down to the R. Jink L then R here, onto the farm track. The track deteriorates slightly then improves again and about 2km after Brackenhow Farm the track emerges into the hamlet of Gaitsgill.

Head straight on, over the bridge, signed 'Raughtonhead / Stockdalewath'. Follow the road for about 0.5km, as it climbs then drops towards Roe Beck. Don't cross Roe Beck but turn L just before the bridge (easy to miss), signed for Skiprigg. Climb and bend R passing a couple of farms then descend to a T-junction. Go R and descend into Stockdalewath to turn L, just before the river, signed 'Highbridge 1'. This lovely, quiet, flat road parallels Roe Beck and enters the hamlet of Highbridge.

B - C In Highbridge bend R to cross the bridge and immediate L to follow the track up to Thistlewood Farm. Go R between the main house and large storage sheds (waymarked with blue arrow on telegraph pole but easy to miss). Shortly the track splits and you follow the L-hand option to cross Roe Beck over a bridge of solid wooden timbers. A very good, straight track now climbs steadily for about 0.5km and ends abruptly in front of a field. Carry on in a straight line, down the R-hand side of the field and through the gate in the far corner to pick up a lovely grassy lane, enclosed by hedges.

Meet a road T-junction opposite Intack House and go R. Descend steeply to cross Roe Beck and climb before the road levels out towards a T-junction. Go R, signed 'Sebergham 3 / Raughtonhead 2½'. Follow this road, with great views on either side, to a T-junction and go L signed for Sebergham and Heskett Newmarket. In just over 1km go R and descend into Churchtown. Go R at the T-junction and follow the narrow road that leads to a church. Go R, just past the cemetery, signed as a bridleway to Bell Bridge. Follow the good track for just over 1km down to Bell Bridge and L to cross the road bridge. Go R at the T-junction over the bridge and climb steeply. Take the first R, signed for Borrans Hill. Pass Lanehead Farm on the R.

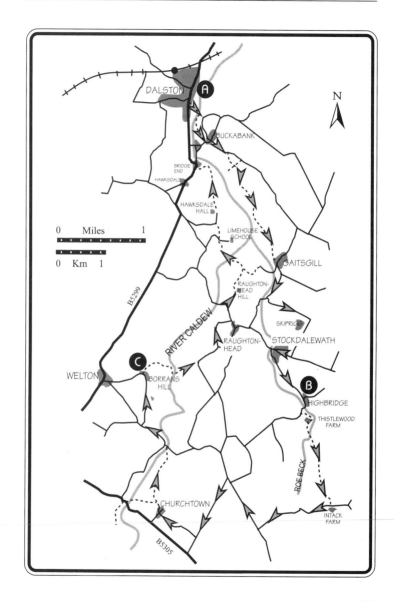

C - A The road bends L by the cluster of buildings that is Borrans Hill. Turn R here and at the immediate split go R, past a farm on the L. Descend the steep, rocky track and pass through a gate into a field. Pass the stone ruins on the R and curve R to come alongside the River Caldew. Go L over Bog Bridge (narrow footbridge with small carry). Go R onto the track over the footbridge, which then bends L and climbs to meet the road at Breconhill. Go L onto the road and at the next fork go L to come to a T-junction by the church in Raughtonhead. Go L, then take the next R, marked for Raughtonhead Hill. Bend L in front of the next set of buildings and the road becomes a track. Bear R at a split just after this and descend to a track T-junction. Go L signed for Hawksdale Hall and Bridge End. Cross over the River Caldew on an impressive iron bridge.

Ascend and follow the track over the tarmac road in front of Lime House School. Follow the grass track and bend L onto a better track to meet a T-junction with a road. Go R, signed for Bridge End, and in about 250m meet the white facade of Hawksdale Hall on the L. Go R here, into gorgeous green pasture and follow the line of the grass track along the L-hand side of this huge field. The track continues through two smaller fields and bends L to meet a tarmac access road for houses. Follow this to the T-junction with the B5299 and go R to descend to the Bridge End Inn. Go R here, over the bridge and take the first L turn. At the T-junction by a bridge on the L turn R and then turn L down the tarmac track on which you left Dalston, to retrace your steps to the centre.

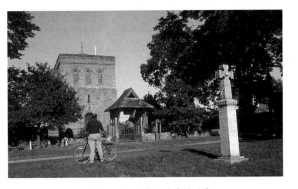

Raughtonhead Church (ride 14)

The grass track near Hawksdale (ride 14)

15 BEWCASTLE FELLS

Start Gilsland village centre   **Grid ref** 633664

Distance 30 km / 18.5 miles

Time Allowed 3 hours   **Off road riding**   46%

Gradient Difficulty *Easy - **Moderate** - Difficult - Very Difficult*

Track Surface / Roads An extremely quiet minor road comes to an end at the bridge before Churnsike Lodge where very good quality track takes over. It stays this way through Spadeadam Forest and descends, with fantastic views over the Bewcastle Fells and beyond, to meet the minor road above Bewcastle at Crossgreens.

OS Maps
1:50,000 Landranger 86 Haltwhistle, Brampton, Bewcastle & Alston
1:25,000 Outdoor Leisure 43 Hadrian's Wall

Access The nearest train stations are at Haltwhistle (9km) and Brampton (13km) on the Newcastle - Carlisle line. You can devise you own link routes using the OS map and if time allows you can take in sections of Hadrian's Wall or the beautiful Lanercost Priory near Brampton.

ALONG THE WAY

• **Gilsland** Border village whose former activities included mining and quarrying. It was even promoted as a spa town in Victorian times; the now Spa Hotel was formerly a convalescent home where people took the water, rich in iron and sulphur. Well-preserved sections of **Hadrian's Wall** are found all around the village and

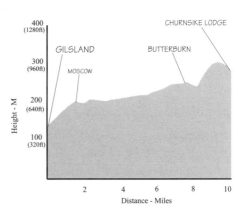

Birdoswald is one of the most impressive Roman forts in the country. The Cumbria Cycle Way between Gilsland and Brampton follows a beautiful straight section of minor road, right alongside Hadrian's Wall. Several pubs, cafe and general store in Gilsland.

• **Spadeadam Waste**, the large upland expanse north of Gilsland, is almost deserted. Where not planted out by the Forestry Commission, for example near Butterburn and Churnsike, it reveals beautiful swathes of grassland, home of rare flora and fauna and dark coloured burns meander their way through this unusual landscape. Much of the area is used by the RAF - TAKE HEED OF THE WARNING NOTICES TELLING YOU NOT TO STRAY FROM THE ROAD AND BE READY FOR SPECTACULAR LOW FLYING JETS ROARING OVERHEAD.

• The magnificent approach to **Bewcastle** reveals a most unusual hamlet, looking rather exposed in a broad sweep of wild moorland. A cluster of residences, farms and a church are grouped around crumbling castle ruins. The **castle** is probably based on an earlier Roman fort, effectively an early warning station for Hadrian's Wall. The Roman fort seems to have been built over an even earlier shrine to a native war god. The present ruins are probably Norman. The **cross** next to the church is Anglo-Saxon and around thirteen hundred years old! The runic inscriptions bear the name of Alcfrith, a sub-king of Northumbria. The **Past & Present** exhibition is housed in the small building in the churchyard and is open 10-8 daily. Interpretive panels give a history of the settlement plus archaeological finds and a mural. The **Lime Kiln Inn** is in Shopford, just south of the church and castle and food is available.

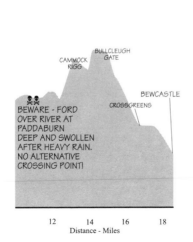

BULLCLEUGH GATE

CAMMOCK RIGG

BEWCASTLE

CROSSGREENS

BEWARE - FORD OVER RIVER AT PADDABURN DEEP AND SWOLLEN AFTER HEAVY RAIN. NO ALTERNATIVE CROSSING POINT!

12   14   16   18
Distance - Miles

Hadrian's Wall near Gilsland (ride 15)

DIRECTIONS

A - B Head west out of Gilsland on the B6318. Cross over the River Irthing and bear R, following signs for Gilsland Spa, Spadeadam and Butterburn. Climb on this road, ignoring the R turn by the church for Gilsland Spa. This road ends at a Ministry of Defence no entry sign (Moscow), but you go R here, onto the road signed as a dead end. Shortly you pass multiple warning signs, the gist of which tell you not to stray off the road because of the danger of unexploded explosives and to look out for low flying aircraft when the red flags are flying!

Simply follow this lovely, lonely road as it passes isolated settlements. Coming alongside the River Irthing at Butterburn ignore the R turn across the bridge to Lampert. The tarmac ends just before a wooden bridge; head over the bridge onto the track, following public / permissive bridleway signs for Paddaburn, Bullcleugh Gate and Bewcastle. By the entrance to Churnsike Lodge go L at the split, following signs for the same destinations.

B - C About 0.5km after that split ignore a R turn and ignore the next R, signed for Paddaburn. Cross a ford (BEWARE - FORD MAY BE 1-2 FT DEEP IN SPATE WITH NO OTHER OBVIOUS CROSSING POINT). Enter the woods and go R at the first split. Simply follow this track through the dense conifers, over Red Sike stream, and climb gradually over Cammock Rigg then descend to the R-hand hairpin over Foulbog Sike, another small stream. Climb steeply away from Foulbog Sike onto open heather moorland.

The track levels out and comes to a T-junction at Bullcleugh Gate, with great views westwards over the Solway Firth. Go R and through the gate. Descend on the main track, ignoring the R split to the army post. Follow red waymarking through several gates on this superb, sweeping track. Descend to Crossgreens cottage and go through the gate to the minor road (track continues over the road as a byroad to Wellington Gate). Go L onto the road here, ignoring the next R to Peel O'Hill. A speedy descent into Bewcastle follows down 'The Strands'.

You can return by the same route or an excellent road route as follows: pass the Limekiln Inn out of Bewcastle (Shopford). It is now a simple matter to use the map to return via Askerton Castle, Banks and the minor road that follows a long and spectacular section of Hadrian's Wall to the north of the River Irthing.

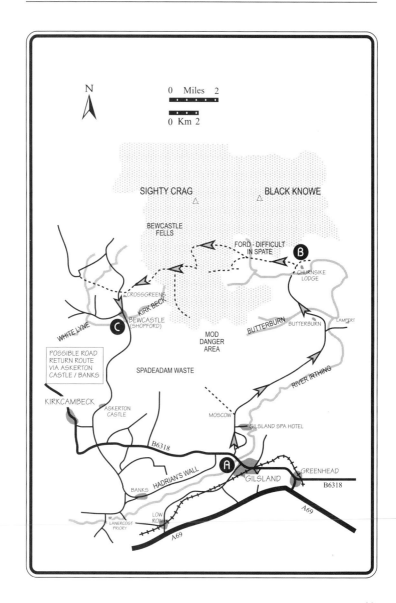

Near Bullcleugh Gate (ride 15)

INDEX OF PLACES
(EXCLUDES DIRECTIONS)

OTHER TITLES

THE ULTIMATE WHITE ROSE ROUTE GUIDE
Out March 2000   *ISBN 1-901464-08-3 £6.95*

104 pages on the Sustrans' Hull - Middlesborough route, taking in the finest Yorkshire scenery. Packed with maps, directions, accommodation and much more.

THE OFFICIAL TRANS-PENNINE TRAIL ACCOMMODATION GUIDE *Out July 2000* ISBN 1-901464-09-1
Please call to confirm price details.

Full accommodation listings with cyclists facilities plus lots of other information.

THE ULTIMATE LONDON-OXFORD CLASSIC Includes
Sustrans' Thames Valley Route. ISBN 1-901464-04-0. £7.95

THE ULTIMATE C2C GUIDE ISBN 1-901464-02-4. £6.95
Sustrans' C2C route - the premier long distance cycle route in the country.

THE ULTIMATE REIVERS ROUTE GUIDE £6.95
ISBN 1-901464-05-9. A more northerly return C2C route.

THE ULTIMATE WEST COUNTRY WAY GUIDE £8.95
ISBN 1-901464-03-2. 250 miles through Cornwall, Devon and Somerset & Avon.

THE ULTIMATE DEVON COAST TO COAST £5.95
ISBN 1-901464-06-7. The Sustran's Ilfracombe to Plymouth via Dartmoor route

YORKSHIRE DALES CYCLE WAY ISBN 1-870141-28-8. £5.50
WEST YORKSHIRE CYCLE WAY ISBN 1-870141-38-5 £4.99
MOUNTAIN BIKING W&S YORKSHIRE ISBN 1-870141-40-7 £5.99
LEISURE RIDES PEAK DISTRICT/DERBS ISBN 1-901464-01-6 £5.95
MOUNTAIN BIKE LANCS / S.PENNINES ISBN 1-901464-00-8 £5.99
BIKING COUNTRY GLASGOW & ENVIRONS ISBN 1-870141-45-8 £5.99

To order any of the above titles please send a cheque, made payable to 'Excellent Books', to the address below and add 50p P&P per book. Free colour catalogue also available on request:

Excellent Books, 94 Bradford Road, Wakefield, West Yorkshire WF1 2AE
Tel / Fax: 01924 315147